D0042105

Books by Ravi Batra

STUDIES IN THE PURE THEORY OF INTERNATIONAL TRADE

THEORY OF INTERNATIONAL TRADE UNDER UNCERTAINTY

CAPITALISM AND COMMUNISM: A NEW STUDY OF HISTORY

MUSLIM CIVILIZATION AND THE CRISIS IN IRAN

The GREAT DEPRESSION of 1990

by

Dr. Ravi Batra

SIMON & SCHUSTER
New York

Copyright © 1987 by Venus Books
Copyright © 1985 by Ravi Batra
All rights reserved
including the right of reproduction
in whole or in part in any form
Published by Simon and Schuster
A Division of Simon & Schuster, Inc.
Simon & Schuster Building
Rockefeller Center
1230 Avenue of the Americas
New York, New York 10020
This is a revised edition of a work originally published under the same title by Venus Books in 1985.
SIMON AND SCHUSTER and colophon are registered trademarks of Simon & Schuster, Inc.
Designed by Irving Perkins Associates
Manufactured in the United States of America
4 5 6 7 8 9 10
Library of Congress Cataloging-in-Publication Data
Batra, Raveendra N.
The great depression of 1990.

"Revised edition"—T.p. verso.
Bibliography: p.
Includes index.
1. United States—Economic conditions—1981–
2. Economic forecasting—United States. 3. Business cycles—United States. 4. Depressions. I. Title.
HC106.8.B39 1987 338.5′42 87-4816
ISBN: 0-671-64022-4

**SUCCESS
IS THE FINAL STEP
ON THE LADDER OF
FAILURE.**

To Sheila and Sunita

CONTENTS

FOREWORD

ANALYSTS CAN basically be divided into two groups when it comes to explaining the course of human history. One group seeks explanations in cyclical regularities; the other seeks explanations in unique events or individuals. Both approaches have their strengths and weaknesses; both can be accused of biases. Those who believe in cyclical regularities are often justly accused of attempting to squeeze unique circumstances into their cyclical interpretations. Those who believe in unique events and individuals are often justly accused of ignoring broad social and economic forces that transcend unique individuals and events.

It is easy to see the appeal of both. If one could find cyclical regularities, the analyst could go beyond descriptions of the past and make predictions about the future. History would come alive as a predictive science. In terms of drama the unique event or person is much more exciting than cyclical regularities. Sudden unpredicted shocks and supermen combine to produce exciting results. Moreover, future events seem to become more controllable. Future history is yet to be made by great individuals and is not dominated by uncontrollable social or economic forces.

It is also easy to see why the two approaches are usually at war with each other. To make its case each side has to argue that the other's prime explanations are of secondary importance. The "great man" to the unique individual school of thought is neither "great" nor "unique" to the cyclical regularities and social forces school of thought. The "cyclical regularities" seen by the analysts who believe in them are neither regular nor cyclical to those who believe in unique individuals or events. What are broad social forces to one become a stew of conflicting minor social forces to the other.

In reality, history is a combination of both elements. The two approaches are not antithetical, and unique events or individuals can be the triggering mechanisms that explode broad social forces or set them off in new directions. For reasons that would probably take a psychiatrist to untangle, it seems difficult for individual analysts, no matter how talented, to combine both approaches. Every analyst in practice tends to focus primarily on one or the other of the two major approaches.

Fortunately it is not necessary for any individual analyst to provide exactly the right judicious mixture of the two approaches. The reader gets that by understanding the explanations of both groups. History is too complicated and has too many facets for any one analyst or approach to reveal all of its complexities.

In seeking to explain inflation and depression Ravi Batra is an analyst of the cyclical school. He seeks to find broad economic or social forces rather than unique events or individuals to explain inflation and depression.

Depression is seen as a product of systematic tendencies for the distribution of wealth to become concentrated among a few. When this happens, demand eventually sags relative to supply and long cyclical downturns commence. Unlike some cyclical analysts Batra believes that such cycles are not inevitable and can be controlled with social policies essentially designed to stop undue concentrations of wealth from developing.

Essentially the economic problem is like that of the wolf and the caribou. If the wolves eat all the caribou, the wolves also vanish. Conversely, if the wolves vanish, the caribou for a time multiply but eventually their numbers become too great and they die for lack of food. Producers need consumers, and if producers deprive workers of their fair share of production income they essentially deprive themselves of the affluent consumers they need to make their facilities profitable. One could think of Batra's argument as a kind of economic ecology where there is a "right" environmental balance.

Inflation is a more complicated problem since it can be seen as either cause or effect. Inflation and changes in the money supply go hand in hand, but which is the cause and which is the effect? The simplest model is one in which an independent decision maker (the government) increases the rate of growth of the money supply and creates inflation. From this perspective there is of course a simple solution. Mistaken policies of printing too much money should be replaced with policies that print less money. One only needs to ask why those directing the government printing presses are from time to time stupid.

In a more complicated model, inflation exogenously occurs (oil and food shocks might get it started, for example) and governments print money to validate the inflation. To not print the money necessary to carry on transactions at the new higher price levels for oil and food would be to cause events—recessions because of falling demand, for example—

which governments are not prepared to tolerate. In this perspective the government technically could prevent inflation, but realistically it politically cannot.

In a still more complicated model, the production of money itself is not under the control of the government. Whatever measure of money the government attempts to control, the market shifts to near substitutes and makes them into what is effectively money. Thus in August 1982 the American Federal Reserve Board announced that it was giving up on its attempts to control the American money supply on the grounds that new money market instruments were being invented so rapidly and in such large numbers that it could not effectively control the money supply. Economic forces had essentially taken over the government's nominal role as printer of money.

Batra's problem is to sort out cause and effect in a money-inflation world where cause and effect are much more complicated than usually believed.

When it comes to the bottom line so beloved of economists, one can learn a lot about events by thinking about them in terms of cyclical regularities, of which Batra gives a novel and brilliant exposition, even if one believes that unique individuals and events are important. Certainly it is unnecessary to agree with all of Batra's conclusions in order to see the appeal of his analysis.

Lester C. Thurow
Professor of Management and Economics
Massachusetts Institute of Technology

PREFACE

EVER SINCE the Second World War, the world has been spared a severe economic crisis. To be sure, there have been a few recessions, some of them severe, but none has displayed the length and ferocity of the Great Depression that afflicted the world in 1929 and lasted more than eight years. I believe that a disaster of the same, if not greater, severity is already in the making. It will occur in 1990 and plague the world through at least 1996.

I have written this book not to scare you, but to warn you of the impending cataclysm. The evidence I will present, including economic data and analysis as well as sociopolitical ideas and historical trends, is overwhelming, and can be ignored only at our own peril. So that you can prepare for the event while there is still time, I will suggest investment strategies to safeguard your assets and carry you and your family through the storm. And finally, I will outline the major changes in government policy that must be implemented to minimize the effects of another great depression.

It is my hope that you will take my warning to heart and begin now to take the steps necessary to ensure your own economic survival. And if my work helps avert the impending crisis in any way, I will cherish this as my lifetime achievement.

1

CAN IT HAPPEN AGAIN?

FEW PEOPLE have any firsthand idea of what a depression is like. The year 1987 marks the fifty-eighth anniversary of the grave economic crisis that began in 1929 and lasted ten years. You would have to be over sixty to really remember what it was like to live through the struggling 1930s.

It all seems remote to the current generation, the baby-boomers and the yuppies, who have grown up in an economic environment where the rate of unemployment has seldom exceeded 10 percent, where the gross national product rises every year, and where salaries rarely decline.

But only two generations ago, the United States was beset by an unprecedented economic disaster that shook the very foundations of Western civilization. The stock market crashed; prices, interest rates, and wages fell like dominoes; and unemployment soared, engulfing 25 percent of the labor force. Suddenly there was mass poverty, and soon thousands were on the verge of starvation. In some cities there were long breadlines and men sold apples on street corners. And all this happened just after the nation's per capita income had reached its highest level in history.

Can it happen again? Can this plague of mass poverty and unemployment afflict our society again? If I say yes, you have a right to be skeptical; but skepticism is healthy, as long as you have an open mind.

In fact, any talk of depression today invites disbelief. Presumably the "great crash" of 1929 was a unique event in our history, and we now have a full array of protective measures to guard against a recurrence. To think otherwise is to be branded a prophet of doom.

I am an economist, trained in scientific analysis, not a sensationalist or a Jeremiah. Yet all the evidence indicates that another great depression is now in the making, and unless we take immediate remedial action the price we will have to pay in the 1990s is catastrophic.

In the pages that follow, I will take you on a historical journey; together we will travel back in time over two centuries of the American economy, explore the empirical evidence surrounding the depressions of the past, and rediscover the age-old axiom that "history repeats itself," although through sharply different institutions and characters.

Basically, repetition of events means that things move in cycles—short, medium, long, and superlong. That is what this book is all about. It will show you how to identify and interpret these cycles, and to recognize how crucial they are to the economic fortunes of us all.

Most ideas reflect needs of the times, and economic theory is no exception. During the Depression decade of the 1930s, economists chiefly sought to explain the deep quagmire that had trapped the system for so long. Some of them explored the business cycle through short-term fluctuations, while others attempted to unravel the long-term waves in business activity. During the relatively stable decades of the 1950s and 1960s, experts turned mainly to esoteric mathematical models designed to refine, and in some cases reformulate, the long-established theories in economics. By then the concept of the business cycle had come to be regarded as obsolete.

However, the 1970s witnessed two major recessions, and with them the old interest in cycles made a comeback. But this time, the problems were far more complex than before, for the recessions were unexpectedly accompanied by persistent inflation. Old theories about economic oscillations were no longer equal to the challenge. Economic forecasts based on outmoded ideas proved wrong so often that at times the economists' sermons invited open skepticism from the public. The puzzle of business cycles, despite myriad attempts to solve it, continues to vex the economics profession.

All the cycles discovered so far by economists have been irregular or intermittent in nature. They display what we call "varying periodicity." Thus the economic literature speaks of a Mitchel cycle which is forty to fifty months long, a Jugular cycle varying from nine to eleven years, a Kuznets-type intermediate cycle of fifteen to twenty-five years, and finally a Kondratieff long-wave cycle lasting anywhere from forty to sixty years. Of all these irregular cycles, none could adequately explain the recessions of the 1970s.

The cycles we shall examine, however, are of a different type. They may be called regular or rhythmical cycles, because their patterns occur at regular intervals. Moreover, some of them deal with variables commonly regarded as "exogenous" or random in economic theory. Money supply is a case in point. It is supposed to be determined by the Federal Reserve System. But it turns out to have had a rhythmical cycle, which can be traced as far back as the birth of the American nation. In all, I shall describe exact patterns in four main economic variables, namely money, inflation, regulation, and depressions. I shall explain them with the help of a socioeconomic and historical theory called the law of social cycles. The time path of these variables has been so exact for so long that it can be projected to form reliable forecasts, both short-term and long-term. In fact, it is this type of historical analysis that in the past has enabled me to make a wide variety of bold predictions.

For example, on December 5, 1978, in a lecture at the University of Oklahoma at Norman, responding to questions raised by an audience of three hundred students and professors, I made the following statements:

1. The Shah of Iran would be overthrown in a revolution in 1979 and the clergy would take over the reins of government.
2. In 1980–81 Iran and Iraq would start a bloody war, which would continue for at least seven years.
3. Europe would experience a serious recession in 1986–87.
4. In 1989–90 America would suffer a depression, which would then turn into an all-time economic disaster plaguing the whole world.
5. Capitalism would be overhauled in the 1990s and so would communism at the turn of the century, culminating in a global golden age.

Two years later, reports of my lecture appeared in two Nashville newspapers that interviewed me just after the Iran-Iraq war, which began in earnest in September 1980.[1]

By then it was evident that the first two of my predictions, all politely ridiculed in 1978, had proved accurate. The Shah of Iran abdicated in January 1979 and the Moslem priesthood, headed by Ayatollah Khomeini, came to power in February of the same year. The Iran-Iraq conflict, already in its seventh year, began in September 1980 and still shows no sign of ending.

As for my third prediction, that too proved to be accurate. In 1986 unemployment rates reached postwar highs in Britain

(13.4 percent) and France (10.5 percent); in Germany, industrial production declined at an annual rate of 6.5 percent in the first two quarters, generating an unemployment rate of 9 percent. Western Europe as a whole suffered an unemployment rate of over 11 percent, signaling a serious recession.

In early 1984, I made additional forecasts of the U.S. economy for 1985 and 1986. My predictions were that the economy would slow down in 1985 and prosper somewhat in 1986, and that inflation, unemployment, and interest rates would either be stable or gradually decline. Energy and farm prices would keep falling, but the stock market would break records in both years.[2]

None of these forecasts has been wrong so far. Moreover, in the first week of January 1986, when I appeared on two talk shows, I made even more forecasts. Alex Burton of KRLD Radio in Dallas asked me to comment on the Dow-Jones Index, which had already risen from 800 in 1982 to about 1500 by the end of 1985. I predicted that the DJI would reach a new high of 2000 by the end of 1986. By December 1986 the Dow had jumped well over 400 points to 1955, and on January 8, 1987 it crossed the 2000 barrier, indicating that my forecast was off by only one week. Walter Evans of CBS local news in Dallas asked me to discuss the tax reform bill, which had been recently rejected by the House of Representatives. My reply was that, despite the current House action, Congress would pass the bill by the end of the year. That bill is, of course, now known as the Tax Reform Act of 1986.

How was I able to foresee the upheaval in the Middle East with accuracy? How was I able to forecast correctly the economic conditions in Europe as well as America? What makes me think that the world is going to face momentous changes in the near future?

I am no astrologer, no psychic. I am an economist and a student of history, and it is my job to make reasoned judgments based on a measurable body of evidence. I have elsewhere explained the analysis underlying my Middle Eastern predictions.[3] The present book examines the reasoning on which my other economic forecasts were based.

The conclusions reached here are derived from an analysis of history and economic theory. My interest in history began in earnest in 1976 when I chanced to read a treatise on society by Prabhat Ranjan Sarkar, a leading scholar from India, who has profoundly enriched the literature of many disciplines, including economics, political science, poetry, psychology, linguistics, art, and, above all, spirituality. As I studied Sarkar's *Human Society,*[4] I was amazed by the scope and depth of his vision. Here finally was an answer to the puzzle of social evolution; here finally was a philosophy of history that in one stroke could unravel the mystery of every social phenomenon. In one compelling doctrine, Sarkar had assimilated the ideas of all past historiographers.

In the next chapter, we will examine in detail what Sarkar calls the law of social cycles. For now I simply wish to describe the process that led me to my seemingly farfetched predictions about the future course of existing societies. Once I grasped the law of social cycles, which claimed universal application, I decided to see for myself if indeed it had been validated by the chronicles of various civilizations. I labored through the history of four different societies—Egyptian, Western, Russian, and Indian—and concluded that each of them had indeed evolved along the pattern described by Sarkar. My inquiry into the human past had by then become all but obsessive. A by-product of that obsession was my work on world history, a book that was completed in 1977 and published the next year.[5] That book explained the theory of social cycles and then demonstrated that the chronicles of the four societies mentioned above fitted precisely into Sarkar's pattern.

The centerpiece of my philosophy of history is an idea

called historical determinism, meaning that history follows a certain pattern, which is observable and which can be used to forecast the future course of events. In my book, after first showing that the four societies had indeed evolved along the social cycles expounded by Sarkar, I went on to predict the future of Western, Russian, and Indian societies. The predictions indicated turmoil, upheaval, and revolutions by the year 2000, unless something was done in time.

In 1978, after completing the book, I turned to the study of other civilizations, notably the Chinese and the Moslem. As an economist I specialize in building esoteric mathematical models of international trade. The word had gotten around about my sudden foray into history and the unusual nature of my conclusions. In November 1978, I received an invitation from the University of Oklahoma economics department to give two lectures on, among other things, the future of capitalism and communism. So it was that on the fifth of December I found myself facing a large audience of students and faculty at Norman.

When I wrote my first book on history, my ideas were still in the formative stage. I had a general view of the future of various societies, but the specifics still eluded me. Even where I felt that a specific event would occur in a particular year, I lacked the confidence to put it in writing. While I had a body of evidence, I did not feel that it constituted sufficient proof.

Shortly after the publication of my work in 1978, Iran experienced a major upheaval. I had expected this all along, but lacked the conviction to include it in my book. By August 1978 the Iranian turmoil was in full swing. There were daily protests and demonstrations by the public, brutally put down by the Shah's police. The tumult in Iran, with all its political and economic ramifications, was the spark I needed to shed my customary caution and declare openly the exact years during which I expected certain events to occur. This I did at the first opportunity that arose—during my lectures at Norman in which I boldly made the five predictions mentioned earlier.

Since then I have gathered new data about the American economy, and now feel that I can prove to others what I have believed and taught my students for so many years. The evidence is extensive, and draws support not only from the law of social cycles but also from a variety of statistics. I am convinced now more than ever before that an unprecedented depression will afflict the American economy, and hence the world economy, around 1990 and last for seven years.

This book builds on the arguments in my two previous books on history, reinforced by my current research, that the dominant variables in the U.S. economy have moved along an exact cycle of three decades. Specifically, I have discovered that, except during the turbulent period following the Civil War, the rate of inflation has reached its peak *every third decade* over the past two centuries. Simultaneously, the rate of money growth has also crested *every third decade* over the same time period. Another variable displaying an identical pattern is the degree of government regulation of the economy. In other words, the peak decades of inflation and money growth also turn out to be the peak decades of government regulation.

These correspondences are extraordinary features of the American economic system. If we ignore for the moment the two decades following the Civil War, we find that the U.S. economy has moved along virtually a predestined path ever since Independence. Regardless of the massive socioeconomic transformations that later occurred, inflation, money growth, and government regulation of business have crested together every third decade.

As for contractions in the economy, the three-decade pattern described above still holds, but with a modification. A steep recession has occurred every decade since the 1780s.

A depression, which is far worse than a recession, occurred every third or sixth decade, in the sense that if the third decade experienced only a recession, then the sixth decade witnessed an economic downturn of crisis proportions.

What will cause the depression of the 1990s? The same forces that precipitated the disaster of the 1930s! Not only are the same forces at work today, but the current U.S. and world economies are further burdened by a heavy load of debt, which did not exist in the 1930s and which is likely to make things much worse in the near future.

Economists generally blame the cataclysm of the 1930s on faulty monetary and fiscal policies of the U.S. government. In fact, the primary cause of that depression, or of any other, has so far eluded the experts. There was nothing new in the monetary and fiscal policies of those times. The government had followed similar policies during previous recessions. What was so different that turned an ordinary recession in 1930 into an unprecedented collapse? The answer lies in the unprecedented concentration of wealth that peaked in 1929. The concentration of wealth is again rising in the 1980s and beginning to assume the menacing levels of the 1920s.

Here's what you can expect in the chapters that follow: In Chapter 2 we'll examine Sarkar's law of social cycles. Chapters 3, 4, and 5 will focus on the long-run cycles of money growth, inflation, and government regulation in the United States. These cycles have followed exactly the same pattern by jointly cresting every third decade, except in the aftermath of the Civil War, when they were all disrupted alike. In Chapter 6 we'll attempt to uncover the pattern underlying the steep recessions and depressions that have periodically convulsed economic and social life. This pattern is not as clear-cut as that of money growth and inflation, but it does exist.

In Chapter 7 we'll assemble all the foregoing evidence to demonstrate that the depression of the 1990s is now all but inevitable. Chapter 8 sets forth a specific step-by-step program that you can implement today to protect your assets and prepare for the crisis now in the making. Finally, Chapter 9 prescribes certain reforms that could be currently followed to prevent or minimize the depression. I earnestly hope that my evidence convinces the government to take some timely steps and enact the needed legislation. Even if the politicians ignore my advice, maybe the very awareness of the coming depression will act to soften its blows. I just pray that my work helps you protect your assets from any coming disaster.

In sounding advance sirens of the coming economic collapse, I am not alone. In an article entitled "The 1929 Parallel" in the January 1987 issue of *The Atlantic Monthly*, John Kenneth Galbraith, one of the world's leading economists, points to the impending stock market collapse and possibly a total economic disaster. In fact, Galbraith notes sardonically, "among those suffering most will be those who regard all current warnings with the greatest contempt."

2

THE LAW OF SOCIAL CYCLES

HOW SOCIETY evolves is a question that has baffled many minds since ancient times. Plato, Aristotle, St. Augustine, Marx, Spengler, and Toynbee, among others, have tried to solve this puzzle, but their ideas, once the cause of much intellectual ferment, hold little appeal for most social scientists. While there is much in their thought that will endure forever, economists today disparage their claims of universality and relevance. Their method of analysis, namely the method of historical determinism wherein the student attempts to detect a pattern in the maze of historical events, is an idea that has long been regarded as dead.

However, P. R. Sarkar has recently revived this idea in terms of a theory called the law of social cycles. Many scholars have tried to discern in the chaos of history a certain rhythm, a subtle harmony complying with natural laws, but their peers, suspicious of any theorizing about apparently arbitrary social phenomena, have scoffed at their views. Sarkar's contribution, as we shall see, is totally different. It does not suffer from those flaws common to other philosophies based on historical determinism.

One reason the idea of historical determinism has traditionally invited so much hostility can be traced to a popular misconception. True, the concept means that history follows a set pattern; that society evolves and undergoes transformations in tune with a discernible rhythm. But it does not imply, as is commonly believed, that humanity cannot make its own destiny; nor does it signify fatalism and resignation before the might of Providence.

All historical determinism means is that, while man indeed is the architect of his own fate, he has to operate within bounds determined by a higher principle: nature. While natural laws cannot be defied, we can work within their perimeters to generate a better environment—a better society. Certainly, water by its nature flows downward. This law can never be reversed no matter how hard we try. But does it mean that the life-giving river flowing down the hills to the plains cannot be tamed and harnessed to our advantage? Of course not. Thus, all historical determinism means is that the arena within which man is free to maneuver is already predetermined by the principle of social evolution. And it is this arena that Sarkar sets out to explain. To him society is a dynamic entity, relentlessly moving, never at rest.

While man is free to decide his own course of action, he faces limits imposed by the society in which he lives. He can determine his own evolution but not social evolution, which, in the interest of order in the universe, must follow the dictates of nature.

THE FOUR SOCIAL CLASSES

It can be safely stated that most social phenomena are in one way or another related to human nature. Thus, Sarkar begins with general characteristics of the human mind. He argues that even though most people have common goals and ambitions, their methods of achieving their objectives may differ from person to person, depending on inner qualities of the individual. Most of us, for instance, seek living comforts and social prestige. But some of us try to attain them by developing intellectual skills, some by developing physical skills, and some by accumulating wealth. Finally, some people have little ambition in life, and they form a class by themselves. Thus, society is basically composed of four types of people, each endowed with a different frame of mind.

People have common objectives, but their modus operandi to attain them differs because of sharp differences in their innate abilities and qualities. Some persons, born with superior bodily strength, excel in physical skills requiring stamina, courage, and vigor. Such people are usually employed in occupations involving physical risks. Sarkar calls them persons of warrior mentality. In his view, soldiers, policemen, fire fighters, professional athletes, skilled blue-collar workers, and the like belong to the class of warriors in the sense that all these occupations require physical skills. Thus, anyone who tries to solve his problems with the help of his might and muscle can be said to have a warrior turn of mind.

There is another type of person who lacks the physical energy of the warrior but is endowed with a relatively superior intellect. Being so endowed, he or she tries to develop mental skills to do well in society. To Sarkar, everyone attempting to solve his problems with the help of his brains rather than brawn is an intellectual. Sarkar's use of the term is much broader than is generally conceived. To him, not just philosophers, writers, and scholars, but lawyers, physicians, poets, engineers, scientists, white-collar workers, and priests are intellectuals because they all utilize their minds rather than muscle power to attain their goals.

There is yet another type of person who, according to Sarkar, strives to accumulate wealth to achieve what is generally regarded as the good life. Such people are also bright, but their minds run mainly after money. They are smarter than the warrior type but not as intelligent as the intellectual. Yet they are usually more affluent than the other two. Such people are called acquisitors, because virtually all their propensities are engaged in amassing wealth. To them money is all that matters in life; it alone is their key to success and prosperity. Merchants, bankers, moneylenders, businessmen, and landlords generally belong to the class of acquisitors. While other classes seek wealth to enjoy material goods, the acquisitor generally covets money for its own sake.

Finally, there is a fourth type of person who is altogether different from the other three. He is the unskilled worker or the physical laborer. He lacks the vigor of the warrior, the brilliance of the intellectual, and the accumulating instinct of the acquisitor. He is also lacking in the high ambition of the other three. His level of education is relatively low, and he is usually deficient in marketable skills. Because of these handicaps the unskilled worker is, and has always been, exploited by the rest of society. He does the work deemed dirty by others, and is the poorest among all classes. Farm workers and unskilled factory workers generally belong to the class of physical laborers.

Exceptions, of course, may be found among those engaged in unskilled occupations. They may be persons of keen intelligence who perhaps perform hard labor not by choice but because of economic necessity or social coercion. Such persons do not belong to the laboring class. Similarly, in virtually all societies in the past slavery was common, and slaves were forced to do servile work. But in no way does that mean that slaves belonged to the class of unskilled workers. The laboring class is simply composed of people who perform physical labor by choice, or because they are unable to acquire technical skills. They lack the initiative, ambition, and drive to succeed in the world; seldom do they shine in society.

These, then, are the four classes which exist in every society and have existed since ancient times in what Sarkar calls the quadri-divisional social system. He differs sharply from those who define classes on economic grounds—on the basis of income and wealth. Sarkar does not neglect the economic aspect, but to him it is only one component among many. Class divisions, in his view, persist because of inherent differences in human nature.

Sarkar's division of society into four classes is by no means inflexible. Social mobility may occur if an individual's mentality changes over time. Through diligent effort, or through prolonged contact with others, a person may move into another class. For example, a laborer may hone his skills to become an accomplished warrior, or through diligence and vigorous education he or she may become an intellectual. Similarly, an intellectual may turn into an acquisitor, or an acquisitor into a laborer. Thus even though class distinctions in society derive from innate differences in human endowments and nature, they may or may not be hereditary.

Yet the possibility of social mobility should not be exaggerated. Although it is possible for a person of one class to acquire the skills of another, it is not easy. A boxer would find it hard to become a scientist, and vice versa. An acquisitor would have the same difficulty in becoming a warrior or an intellectual. But the point is that it is not impossible.

Wherever civilization developed, a careful examination of its history reveals the existence of the four-pronged division of society sketched by Sarkar. His categories of mind are broad enough to cover the full range of a mature society.

Thus every civilization, which is what a mature society is, consists of four classes, each comprising people reflecting the predominance of a certain type of mind. Although individual behavior might display two, or even all, of the four mental attitudes, for the most part, and especially under duress, only one of them predominates. There is a bit of acquisitive instinct in most of us, but only a few make money the consuming obsession of their lives. We are all after a comfortable living standard and social prestige, but some of us attain them by means of physical skills, some through intellectual pursuits, and some by ceaselessly chasing after money. In this order, we are warriors, intellectuals and acquisitors. Largely left behind are the laborers, imbued with little ambition or drive, wanting in basic education and essential skills.

In every society, generally warriors maintain law and order, intellectuals supply philosophy and religion, acquisitors are adept at managing the economy, and laborers do the unskilled jobs.

Although some people display two or more mentalities—for instance, an accomplished army general may also be a superb writer, or an intellectual may also have the great business sense of an acquisitor—such individuals are rare, constituting an exception to the rule. Even in such exact sciences as physics and chemistry, exceptions to physical laws exist and are generally ignored. The laws of economics and society I will develop in this work also tend to disregard the exceptions.

The Law of Social Cycles

In accordance with his quadri-divisional social system, Sarkar argues that a society evolves over time in terms of four distinct eras. Sometimes warriors, sometimes intellectuals, and sometimes acquisitors dominate the social and political scene. Laborers never hold the reins, but at times the ruling class becomes so self-centered and corrupt that a large majority of the people are reduced to poverty. The general public, engaged mostly in making a living, has then little time left for the finer aspects of life—art, music, adventure, poetry, spirituality. Such a time may be called the age of laborers.

No single group, however, can exercise social supremacy forever. What is more interesting, as well as intriguing, is that the movement of society from one epoch to another follows a definite pattern. Specifically, in the development of every civilization, ancient or modern, Oriental or Occidental, "the era of laborers is followed by the era of warriors, the era of warriors by the era of intellectuals, and the era of intellectuals by the era of acquisitors culminating in a social revolution—such a social evolution is the infallible Law of Nature."[6]

This is Sarkar's law of social cycles. Note the word *evolution.* This law of nature is "infallible" because it is based on the evolutionary principle. Just as human evolution is indisputable, just as the onward march of humanity cannot be arrested, so are social cycles an inevitable natural phenomenon, where social supremacy shifts from one class to another, from the collectivity of one type of mind to another. Thus, underneath the seemingly haphazard change in society lies the invisible but unmistakable imprint of nature. Social evolution goes hand in hand with human evolution.

It is in such sweeping terms that Sarkar conveys his message. To him society is a dynamic entity and perpetual change is its essence. A civilization emerges with the rise of warriors, and after considerable ups and downs through the eras of intellectuals, acquisitors, and laborers, it goes back to the warrior age, only to resume its evolutionary march in tune with the same old rhythm. This, in short, is Sarkar's law of social cycles.

The Era of Laborers

How do we recognize the era of laborers? The laboring society is one that suffers from complete lack of guidance, leadership, and authority; one where the so-called leaders become so egocentric and greedy that the majority of people, following in their footsteps, display a mentality ruled by instinctive behavior, greed, and total self-concern. The era of laborers, then, is characterized by near anarchy, by a lack of social order. Family ties are not binding, people scorn higher values and the finer things of life, morals are extremely loose, crime is rampant, and materialism permeates society to the core. All laborer societies in ancient times were primitive, and remained primitive until some warriors emerged and wrested the leadership into their own hands. However, later laborer eras were actually governed by acquisitors and can be properly called "acquisitive-cum-laborer" eras. I shall further explain this point shortly in this chapter.

What distinguishes a civilization from a primitive community is a matter of controversy among historians. Sarkar's division of society into four classes in accordance with their mental characteristics suggests a straightforward definition. Using his concepts, we can say a primitive society is one where all its members display laboring mentality, so that it has little chance of growing out of the chasm of ignorance and savage existence. The rise of civilizations may then be ascribed to the rise of persons with non-laboring mentality, especially those endowed with warriorlike qualities.

One way to differentiate between laborers and other groups is to look at their levels of education. In general, schooling is highest among intellectuals and lowest among the unskilled, with warriors and acquisitors standing somewhere in the middle. In many societies in the past, only priests had the ability to read and write. Access to education was considered a privilege, of which the laboring peasants and unskilled workers were totally deprived. Today education is available to all, yet laborers remain relatively the least educated.

Of one issue there is little doubt. The early history of humankind, the prehistoric or Paleolithic period—covering the time of *Homo habilis* to Java man, to Neanderthal man, and finally to our immediate ancestor, Cro-Magnon man—belongs to the laborer era, which may be traced back to 1,750,000 B.C., when Paleolithic man is supposed to have evolved enough from the apes to perform what anthropologists deem to be astonishing feats. There is some evidence that Neanderthal man and Cro-Magnon man, who lived in caves, had begun to cook their food and bury their dead. Group life, which is traceable to the Lower Paleolithic culture, had become more organized with the advent of Cro-Magnon men. Their highest achievement, however, was in art; some of their cave paintings are extant today, giving us an idea of daily life in the Upper Paleolithic culture.

Although group life had been established during the Paleolithic age, the essentials of an organized society were still absent. The institution of marriage and family life was yet to evolve. Men and women lived together not in a morally and legally binding relationship, but purely because of biological attraction to each other. They felt little love for their own children, much less for their fellow beings. Each powerful man had several females: being less strong than men, women had to accept an inferior status. Since there was no government, there was no law and order; there was anarchy, with everyone preoccupied with self-preservation.

Today, over the eons, we have evolved to the extent that a relapse to the prehistoric culture, to that savage existence, is inconceivable. Can we then say that humanity cannot now degenerate into a laborer era? The answer is no.

Everything in this world is relative, changing with respect to time and place. A laborer society today would be similar in some respects to its counterpart in prehistoric times, but it could not be exactly the same; that would be negating millions of years of natural evolution. The laborer mind is now much more intelligent than it was at the birth of human consciousness; no longer need it be passive in the absolute sense. A laborer today is one with low initiative and drive relative to people of the other classes. And for this reason the laboring class is exploited as much today as in the past. Its toil is still indispensable to the survival of any society, but ruling classes are taking advantage of it everywhere in the world.

The distinctive feature of a laborer society today would be the open disregard of governmental authority and law by its dominant members. Thus, unlike the Paleolithic age, government may exist in a contemporary laborer society, but its rule would not be respected; violent crime would become rampant, with people living in fear. In ancient times there were no family ties worthy of the name. Today, the weakening of family bonds would be reflected in the lack of discipline of children and their disrespect for parental authority, in frequent divorces and marital violence, and in the heartless removal of the elderly from the family. Women had a lowly status in the distant past; in a contemporary laborer society, such inferior status would be manifested in a high incidence of prostitution, pornography, and general exploitation of women by men.

In short, if these characteristics are prevalent in a society, it is unmistakably languishing in the laborer era. A close scrutiny of history reveals that all civilizations occasionally pass through such periods, when, for example, they are beset by internal fissures or external assaults. Actually the difference between the extinct and existing civilizations is simply that the former were overwhelmed by the ills of a laborer era, whereas the latter overcame them to resume their forward march of evolution.

THE ERA OF WARRIORS

The era of warriors, in terms of political and social structure, is diametrically opposite to the era of laborers. In the warrior age the army, headed by a dictator—king, emperor, president—controls the government as well as society. Political authority is centralized in the form of an absolute government, people are highly disciplined, family ties are morally binding, women are well respected, and so on. Intellectuals and acquisitors enjoy some respect in the warrior age, although they have little say in governance. But laborers perform the physical labor for the warrior class, and in the closing stage of this period, as in that of every other era, they are mercilessly exploited. However, at the dawn of the warrior age, the ruler respects their contribution and treats them with care and compassion. Laborers, though physically strong, lack the enterprising and adventurous spirit of the warriors, who use their physical skills to advance in life, to excel within their circle. It is this spirit which enabled Columbus to discover America, Robert Peary to reach the North Pole, Edmund Hillary and Tenzing Norkay to climb Mount Everest. Propelled by the same spirit, the Russians launched a Sputnik and the Americans set their footprints on the moon.

A warrior believes in physical discipline, in firm authority over his family, and when he comes to power, his family extends to the entire population living in his domain. A warrior ruler believes in authoritarian government, in absolute power. That is why warrior eras have always been characterized by political centralization, by the divine right of kings, and by dictators.

The warrior era began with the Neolithic period, or New Stone Age, which seems to have been established by 3000

B.C., although in Egypt it had emerged by as early as 5000 B.C. The Neolithic period is marked by the beginning of agriculture and the domestication of animals. Men and women began to emerge from caves and attain some measure of mastery over their environment. What else but an adventurous spirit could have inspired them to go out and look for dependable sources of food? This was a major change, for up until that time man had been only a food gatherer, but Neolithic man became a food producer.[7]

Another distinct feature of this period was the rise of institutions, for which a highly organized group life is essential. The origin of the state may also be ascribed to this period, when the discovery of agriculture and the subsequent population explosion made social organization indispensable to survival.

Although traces of Neolithic culture can be observed in places even today, it is supposed to have ended when metal was discovered. In Egypt it terminated as early as 4000 B.C., and in Europe by 2000 B.C. In most other parts of the world, such as the Middle East and Persia, where primitive societies were replaced by ancient civilizations, the Neolithic age came to an end around 3000 B.C. However, the warrior era seems to have continued with few interruptions, although in accordance with general human evolution, it underwent drastic changes. In order to distinguish the earliest warrior epoch of a society from the later ones, a distinction important in any discussion of ancient civilizations, the Neolithic period may be called the tribal warrior age.

In the immediate post-Neolithic age, the warrior era is represented by the autocratic rule of kings, emperors, and dictators. Ancient Egypt, the Rig-Vedic age in India, ancient Greece, ancient Rome, and ancient Persia are prime examples of societies where a distinction needs to be made between the tribal and the subsequent imperial warrior age.

In the warrior age, the insistence on discipline, first in the family and then in society, is extremely strong, and for this reason women enjoy high social status, at least higher than their stature in other eras. In the Neolithic period, the tribes were led by great fighters. Being constantly at war with one another, they soon discovered the importance of numerical strength. Fast growth of population thus became their common objective, an undertaking in which women were equal partners. On this account, and to ensure that reproduction was restricted to within the group, brave and daring women were honored as group mothers in Neolithic times. Thus the early warrior society was governed by a matriarch who provided lineal identity to every man and woman belonging to a particular clan.

The institution of marriage first emerged in the tribal warrior age. In the laborer era there was hardly any marital life. Men and women lived together purely because of biological needs. Consequently children did not know who their father was, but everyone knew who the mother was. This is another reason why women enjoyed greater respect in those times, and why, when civilization first sprouted from the soil of primitive society, group mothers became the leaders.

Once society was organized into tribes, men and women began to feel a bond in their conjugal relations. The father came to have a sense of duty and responsibility toward his offspring. Consequently, woman's burden in raising children declined to an extent, and with this began the decline in her social status as well. Gradually families began to be dominated by men. In time, matriarchy gave way to patriarchy, wherein the tribal head was a man and descent was recognized in his name. How long the group mothers dominated society cannot be easily ascertained, but it appears that patriarchy had emerged before the end of the Neolithic period. As women's influence declined, men began to have many wives toward the close of the tribal warrior age.

In Paleolithic times there were also frequent wars among

the people, but they were initiated solely by self-preservation, with warriors and laborers fighting together for their own survival. Whereas laborers had fought for food and shelter, warriors fought for dignity and self-esteem as well—a mentality heralding a warrior age. In time, the warrior rulers became highly authoritarian; they lost much of their early benevolence, and as a result laborers were mercilessly exploited. Their domains also expanded greatly; many tribes were unified after lengthy warfare into a vast empire headed by the conqueror. In the holocausts the warriors unleashed, laborers were the helpless participants. And for what? For the ego gratification of the megalomaniac warrior who craved supremacy over the entire world. In most warrior societies, the bloody wars of conquest portended the end of warrior domination and the birth of an era of intellectuals, who, represented by the priesthood or court ministers, came to power in every civilization at the end of the warrior age.

The Era of Intellectuals

The despotic governments of the warrior age were fundamentally unstable, for nothing based on fire and sword can command obedience from the people for long. For that reason, absolute rulers felt the need for justifications to support their arbitrary rule. In this they were ably assisted by the intellectuals, who devised cunning theories to justify the ruler's absolute authority over his people. Thus were born such concepts as the infallibility of monarchs and the divine right of kings. That is why in the heyday of the warrior age the intellectuals enjoyed a social status second only to warriors. And when the authority of absolute rulers declined as a result of endless wars, the leadership vacuum could be filled only by men of knowledge who alone commanded enough respect and authority at the time. Everywhere we find that intellectuals came to power in the aftermath of protracted warfare. In the West, for instance, the Catholic Church rose to primacy after the fall of the militaristic Roman Empire.

The intellectual is endowed with foresight and keenness of mind. In general an intellectual is cautious and pragmatic; he or she relishes comfort but not at the cost of physical labor. Consequently, the intellectual attains power only by defeating the warrior in a battle of wits. Intellectuals rule indirectly—through their control over the warrior ruler who alone can summon the might to keep order in society. Whenever and wherever the intellectuals perceived that their time had come, they devised new dogmas rationalizing their hold over the people. First they managed to convince the warrior of the possibility of his eternal damnation after death, and then concocted rituals so complex that he was forced to seek their counsel. These the intellectuals were more than glad to provide in exchange for political power and creature comforts.

After outwitting the warrior, the intellectuals then set out to inject baseless fears and prejudices in other classes as well. Once the ruler was won over, it was just a matter of time before the rest of society yielded to their self-serving doctrines. Thus we find that in nearly every civilization the people were once caught in the stranglehold of power exercised by priests, court ministers, or other manipulators surrounding the ruler.

The structure of government in the era of intellectuals appears to change little from that prevailing in the warrior age, except that now, because of the weakness of the ruler, the real authority is exercised by someone behind the scenes. Yet the intellectuals need the warriors to maintain their control over the general public, and, therefore, the government is now somewhat decentralized. The apparent ruler is no longer absolute, nor is the indirect ruler.

The early warrior period, as noted before, was marked by matriarchy, a social order in which group mothers dominated; this was followed by patriarchy, in which the male head of the tribe became supreme; and finally came the absolute rulers. Throughout the warrior era women continued to enjoy respect in society, were regarded as man's helpmate, and commanded sufficient, if not equal, social prestige.

In the era of intellectuals, however, woman came to be regarded as inherently inferior to man. In the warrior era, at least in its first half, the warrior's manliness enabled him to treat women on a more or less equal footing with men. An intellectual, however, lacks the warrior's courage, and consequently is always afraid of insubordination by other groups. He has to be, lest the muscular warriors and laborers see through his shaky dogmas and cast him aside. Thus an intellectual, in order to rule, will always try to subjugate other groups.

After besting the warrior in the intellectual arena, the male victors then proceeded to bind women, restricting their every freedom; the web was even tighter than that binding men. In many societies, women were denied access to scriptures as well as to secular education. In some cases their subservience to men came close to slavery. The husband was, and in some cases still is, considered the wife's master. Today, we find it hard to believe that even in the West, which had supposedly shaken off dogmatic irrationalism after the Middle Ages, women were deprived of voting rights as late as the twentieth century.

True, women have by now come a long way in attaining freedom and equality, but the idea of woman as inherently inferior, as property, as a plaything of men persists in many parts of the world. Woman's humiliation, however, began only with the intellectual era, and if it has endured so long the blame rests squarely with men of the intellectual class. In line with the general double-talk of such men, in theory woman was accorded a status equal to man, but the reality was something very different.

It was also in the era of intellectuals that prostitution came into being. Credit for its birth goes solely to the priests and other intellectuals who made women totally dependent on men. Without a husband, a woman economically became a cripple; prostitution presumably began when widows or other women could not find husbands, and there was no other recourse. The degradation was sanctioned, moreover, by priestly pressures on virgins to dedicate themselves to the service of temple gods. This is how the so-called temple prostitution developed in ancient communities of Egypt, Greece, and India, among others. In Paul Lacroix's vivid words:

> As soon as religions had been born from the fear inspired in the heart of man by sight of the great commotions of nature, as soon as the volcano, the tempest, the thunderbolt, the earthquake and the angry sea had led him to invent gods, prostitution offered herself to those same terrible and implacable deities, and the priest took for himself an offering from which the gods represented would have been unable to profit. . . . Prostitution became, from then on, the essence of certain cults of gods and goddesses who ordained, tolerated or encouraged it. Hence sprang the mysteries of Lampascus, of Babylon, of Paphos and of Memphis; hence the infamous traffic which was carried on at the gates of temples; hence those monstrous idols with which the virgins of India prostituted themselves; hence the obscene dictatorship which the priests arrogated to themselves under the auspices of their impure divinities.[8]

THE ERA OF ACQUISITORS

Nothing irrational or illogical can endure forever. The web in which the intellectuals caught the rest of society began to loosen as other classes slowly saw through their manipulations. Quite fittingly, and perhaps ironically, some elements within the intellectual class itself began to question the priests' intentions. Not only the elaborate rituals but also the luxury and corruption of the priesthood came under fire. Among the intellectuals themselves there also occurred a good deal of argument and doctrinal battles, and those who were thus defeated started accumulating wealth to compensate for their intellectual debility. Similarly, some warriors also followed that route. In this way, another mentality evolved in human beings; another class, one obsessed with money—the acquisitive mind.

In the meantime, all forms of authoritarianism—secular as well as ecclesiastic—were being challenged by certain intellectual reformers. New philosophies of individualism, of the inherent rights of man, were gradually sinking into the public consciousness. Such philosophical pillars of the state as the doctrine of the divine right of kings were being fatally undermined. As a result of all these developments, the power base slowly drifted toward the wealthy class of acquisitors, and thus began the acquisitive age.

In all civilizations, the acquisitive class consisted of the rich, belonging to such diverse groups as landlords, money lenders, and merchants. No longer was it enough to have a keen intellect to attain comforts and political power. Instead, social prominence rested on one's wealth.

An acquisitor differs from an intellectual mainly in the way he uses his intellect. The latter, while interested in comfortable living and material acquisition, is inclined to intellectual pursuits for their own sake; he likes theorizing about the world. The acquisitor will have none of this; his intellect is obsessed with amassing, not just enjoying, wealth. It is this mentality that reigns during the acquisitive era. Yet the intellectuals have an important role to play. They now help the acquisitors stay in power by doing what they do best—devising dogmas that, in return for some compensation, justify the supremacy of the ruling class. This they accomplish, as always, in a way that lures the gullible—by concealing their support for the acquisitors' primacy behind proclamations of individual rights, liberty, and justice. In reality, however, such lofty principles are openly violated. They are usually observed only when it serves the interests of the affluent. Once the intellectuals give in, warriors and laborers also perform services for the rich. Thus in the acquisitive age, all other classes submit to the wealthy, who then control the means of production—land, factories, capital. Feudalism and capitalism are two pointed examples of acquisitive eras in Western civilization.

Of all forms of government, the one loved by the acquisitor is that in which the central authority is the weakest. In the warrior era this is impossible. In the intellectuals' era, the central power is not so strong, but the rigid social codes that the intellectuals contrive to control people keep a tight leash on would-be acquisitors. That is why one finds that the acquisitive era, especially as it matured, was accompanied by a high degree of decentralized political authority in every civilization. A centralized system can, if it suits its purpose, force the rich to share their wealth with the poor, and no one is more aware of this risk than the acquisitors. Therefore, whenever the wealthy hold the reins, the system of government as well as the administrative apparatus is decentralized over time.

One distressing feature of the epoch of the acquisitor is that the acquisitive mentality eventually infects all sections of society. Attitudes of the ruling class do not spread so much, do not become so pervasive, in other eras; but in the age dominated by the wealthy, other groups ultimately submit to the allure of money. Everything is commercialized as a result—music, art, literature, sports.

Crime also begins to flourish. A general disregard for the

rule of law developed in all acquisitive periods, plaguing the public in every civilization. Family ties eroded; noblemen kept harems; divorce and prostitution increased.

Prostitution, which was born in the era of intellectuals, undergoes a remarkable growth in the acquisitive age. Those who have money to burn are able to corrupt poverty-stricken women. And once the ruling class casts off moral scruples, other classes are quick to follow suit. As a consequence, moral degeneration comes to pervade the entire society. Erosion of family ties, excessive stress on individualism, and a general lack of social discipline spring inevitably from a decentralized political structure.

As time passes, increasing amounts of wealth end up in the hands of the rich, and the acquisitive era gradually drifts toward the lawlessness of the laborer age. Eventually, things become so wretched that angry warriors and intellectuals rise in rebellion and with the help of laborers bring an end to the age of acquisitors. Soon afterward, the rebellious warriors take over and the civilization moves afresh on the track of social cycles.

THE PROCESS OF SOCIAL CHANGE

Sarkar's law of social cycles states that power and influence shift from one class to another in accordance with a certain pattern. Several questions come to mind at this point. First, is the change from one era to another smooth and peaceful, or is it violent and marked by bloodshed? Second, does the rise and fall of a class occur in perceptible stages within each era? Is the rise or fall linear or subject to cycles as well?

It should be noted at the outset that every entity, however small or large, is subject to cycles. Everything in the universe, no matter how short or long its life, moves in ups and downs.

Nothing moves in a straight line. Everybody can see this in his own life. One day a person is happy, another day unhappy. Things are going well today, they may go sour tomorrow. Everything in the world is subject to fluctuations.

The shift in power and prestige from one class to another itself represents the cyclical movement of society. But within each era the dominating class is also subject to oscillations. The class in command may be temporarily dethroned, but if its attitudes continue to prevail among the people, then it will soon come back to power. For example, suppose society is passing through the acquisitive age. Suddenly there is a military coup and the army takes over the government. If the acquisitive mentality continues to dominate the society, soon the wealthy will return to prominence. Thus, within each era, the reigning class's fortunes are subject to cycles. But in any age, named according to the dominant class, that class stays in power much longer than any other. A close analysis of civilizations reveals that during any era the dominant class remains on top for at least two-thirds of that period. For instance, if an intellectuals' era lasted for three hundred years, one would find that during that period intellectuals ruled for at least two hundred years and other groups for at most one hundred years.

Because of overlapping transitional periods, one may not be able to recognize a particular epoch of any society. The fact that nothing moves in a straight line does present difficulties. But a serious student should be able to see where a society stands at any moment in time. The following points should be borne in mind in the study of history:

1. In any society spread over several regions, one should first identify the most important region. For instance, in Western civilization, which is spread among many nations, America today is the most influential country. Since the United States is now passing through the acquisitive-cum-laborer age, which is marked by high crime, extreme materialism, generally loose morals, and excessive individualism, we can say that the entire Western world is in this age. It is possible that some regions of a society may differ from the most important region. But that is not significant. What counts is the dominant mentality in the dominant region of a society. For instance, Canada, another member of Western civilization, is also in the acquisitive age, but it does not suffer from high crime. However, the character of Western society as a whole is determined not by the ruling mentality in Canada, but by that in the United States.

2. There may be more than one important region in a society at any given time. Then the class ruling in the majority of such regions determines the character of that society.

3. Once dominant regions in a society have been identified, the next step is to see which group is in power in those regions. Normally one should be able to pinpoint the class controlling the government, either directly or indirectly. That is, one should be able to see if warriors, intellectuals, or acquisitors command political power. For instance, a centralized government with absolute authority usually means that either warriors or intellectuals are at the helm. If it is not clear which group dominates politics, one should examine the ideology popular in the society. Does it favor a warrior attitude of adventure and fearlessness, or an intellectual's otherworldliness and preference for theory over action, or an acquisitor's materialism over the intellectual or adventurous pursuits of mind?

4. Another way to identify an era in society is to observe what the average person admires most, which careers earn the greatest status, what the popular culture glorifies. Does the common man seek a career in the army, or does he want to become a poet, priest, or statesman, or does he aspire to be a big landlord, banker, merchant, or businessman? In any society the profession of the ruling class is the one most sought by the public. In a warrior age, the average man generally dreams of becoming an army officer. In an era of intellectuals, he aspires to become an influential thinker, a theologian, or a high-placed political adviser. In an acquisitive age, he seeks to become a merchant, businessman, landlord, or financier. In a laborer age, people usually become lazy, extremely materialistic, and greedy. They want to become wealthy without working hard.

Each era moves through five stages—infancy, youth, maturity, senility, and death. During infancy and senility, the ruling group faces many challenges and may be temporarily thrown out of power. But during youth and maturity, there is social and political stability, the government is relatively benevolent, and society evolves at a fast pace. However, successive generations of the dominant class, having been nurtured in luxury, turn oppressive and tyrannical. They care nothing for the rights of the people. New conflicts develop in society, and the fortunes of the rulers begin a long-term decline. Old age sets in and the era meets its end, frequently, though not always, by violent upheaval. Those opposing the ruling class then come to power and begin a new era, with different ideology and attitudes.

This is the process that manifests itself time and again in the course of social evolution from the warrior era to the intellectuals' era to the acquisitive era. Whereas in all phases of civilization, society consists of four broad classes, at the end of the acquisitive era only two remain: acquisitors and laborers—warriors and intellectuals having been reduced to the laboring class by the extreme concentration of wealth. For a long time in the acquisitive era, the standard of living remains high and the other classes make their living by providing services to the affluent. For a while, the entire social order works to support the dominance of the rich. The concentration of wealth continues apace, but since material resources available to society are limited, the acquisitors grow richer and richer at the expense of other classes.

It is at this juncture that another age of laborers is born. However, it is more appropriate to call this new laborer era an acquisitive-cum-laborer age, because now there is some degree of power sharing between acquisitors and laborers. While the acquisitors still retain positions of power, they cannot dismiss the concerns and strengths of the now organized laborers. Thus the term "acquisitive-cum-laborer age" describes a society existing toward the end of the age of acquisitors.

As wealth becomes concentrated, the living standard of the other three classes progressively declines, until there comes a time when society degenerates into two groups—the haves and the have-nots. So strong is the power of want and hunger that the distinctive features of the warrior's and intellectual's minds submit to the compulsions of survival. It is during such dark days that the acquisitive-cum-laborer age comes into being. The resultant crime, poverty, and malaise eventually invite the revolt of the masses, who are led by the very warriors and intellectuals—now diminished to laborer ways of thinking—who had once embraced the acquisitive system with open arms. Sarkar calls this upheaval the laborer revolution, one that occurs in the terminal phase of the acquisitive era, contributes to its end, and is brought about by disgruntled warriors and intellectuals.

The laborer revolution reflects not the fact that it is engineered by the laborer class, which is generally unable to lead, but the fact that it is masterminded by those reduced to the laborer's level of poverty. Few warriors and intellectuals then remain, for, forced to devote all their time to making a living, they have little time for other pursuits. The laborer revolution sweeps aside the influence of wealth. In the ensuing society, which may arise immediately or after a brief period of adjustment, power reverts to the warriors.

WESTERN SOCIETY

Let us now explore the annals of Western society to see if it has indeed evolved in terms of the law of social cycles.

Students of Western civilization generally begin its study with the Greco-Roman era, although some trace it back to the Minoan period on the island of Crete and then to the Neolithic age in Europe. Proponents of the latter view are, however, in a minority, for earlier civilizations were strikingly different, and in any case there is not much known about the ancient European world. Let us then begin with the Christian era.

To understand the evolution of the West, it is necessary to have some background on the social structure of the Roman Empire, because even though that empire has long been dead, Roman law, Latin literature, and some other Roman institutions have survived till this day. At the dawn of the first century A.D., the warrior era can be seen as prevailing in the empire, with Augustus as its emperor enjoying supreme command over the vast Roman provinces. It is an age of absolute rule, and the tradition of conquest continues unabated. The chief bequest of the so-called Principate, said to have begun with the ascendance of Augustus, is Roman law, which, among other things, affirmed that all humans are by nature equal and have certain fundamental rights that no government is entitled to transgress.

The absolute rule of the emperors reached its zenith in A.D. 284 with the accession of Diocletian. Prior to his reign, the ruler, in theory if not in fact, was an agent of the people, who had some fundamental rights, but now even that semblance of "responsible" government disappeared. The main reason for this change lies in the economic decline of the third century; the people were so demoralized they were ready to forfeit their rights for the elusive hope of peace and security.

Despotism, however, could only temporarily arrest the downfall of the Roman Empire, whose economic and social structure had already been enfeebled by the decline in agriculture and commerce. The lack of a law of succession periodically gave rise to bloody conflicts at the time of the ruler's death, and the resulting degeneration of the army only accentuated the decay. It was at this time that the Christian religion gained a foothold. The Catholic Church succeeded because it provided guidance and shelter to the oppressed at a time when the empire was crumbling under the weight of imperialism as well as invading hordes who struck from all directions—northern Europe, the Eurasian Steppes, the Arabian Peninsula, North Africa.

In accordance with Sarkar's law of social cycles, the church in any case would have inherited power from the Roman Empire, but the downfall of the empire was hastened by the onslaught of barbarian invasions, bringing bloodshed, pillage, and chaos. Had it not been for Christianity, Western civilization would have met its end at that time; under the spate of invading marauders, the decadent Roman society would have died were it not for a little life-breath that vibrated the budding church. This is how the era of intellectuals, represented by the pope and bishops, was born.

At first, of course, Christianity had to struggle against tremendous odds. It is true that the old pagan religions were losing ground during the first three centuries, but this did not necessarily spell triumph for the religion of Christ. The imperial government either supported or tolerated many other cults and beliefs from the East. However, with the decline of the social order, Christianity, in spite of tough competition from other religions, spread quickly, and by the time of Diocletian, Christian communities were organized in nearly every city of the empire. Even the periodic official persecution of Christians could only slow, but not stop, the eventual triumph of Christianity. Most of its early converts came from the slave and laboring classes.

In the first three centuries, Christianity genuinely embodied the teachings of Christ, whose magnetic and selfless life story dominated the preachings. This was the main source of strength in the admirable lives led by the early saints. With the passage of time, however, especially after Christianity was recognized as the official religion of the empire toward the end of the fourth century, the church too succumbed to luxury and corruption. Having gained official recognition, the church was no longer a haven for the poor and oppressed. In order to acquire wealth and power, it subordinated principles to political expediency. The bishops were more interested in perpetuating their privileges than in living up to sublime and lofty ideals. Instead of society depending on the church for moral guidance, the church became a parasite on society.

During the latter part of the fourth century, the church gained ground because the emperor Constantine had been converted to Christianity. This was a marked reversal from the older days of persecution, because now the ruler himself encouraged enrichment of the priesthood. By the fifth century, the clergy had become the dominant social and even political power of the empire. In the name of the warrior king, it was the church—Pope, bishops, and priests—that ruled society. The age of intellectuals thus began in the fifth century. At the behest of the clergy, the government now acted to root out paganism, its rituals and sacrifices, although later the church itself felt it necessary to devise elaborate rituals of its own.

The intellectuals' age in the West lasted from the middle of the fifth century to about the end of the ninth. During these four hundred years, priests completely controlled society, with only periodic opposition from the warriors. One such warrior was the emperor Charlemagne, who reigned from 768 to 814. Charlemagne not only conquered many territories, but also took over the church, thereby temporarily establishing an era of warriors. Other than that, the clergy had few rivals for more than four centuries. The priest derived his authority from the dogma portraying him as an intermediary between man and God. This is precisely how intellectuals govern. Their theories enable them to trap society in a complex web of self-serving rules and regulations.

With the emergence of the intellectuals' age, women lost the high social status they had enjoyed during the Roman Empire. During the preceding age of warriors, women had participated in social, economic, and political events. But as soon as the priesthood took over, a woman came to be regarded as inherently evil, a temptress. Man's purpose was to serve God, and woman's to serve man. Priests were not sure if woman had a soul, and proclaimed man to be master of his wife. One effect of these attitudes was that rape and prostitution became solely the fault of woman.[9] And in this respect what happened in Western society was repeated in all civilizations.

The intellectuals' age lasted until the end of the ninth century, when a series of events led to the ascendancy of the landlords, culminating in feudalism. The rule of intellect then gave way to the rule of wealth. Intellectuals became subservient to the landlords, who possessed the acquisitive mentality. The intellectuals justified the supremacy of landed magnates in terms of a new theory called the Christian paternalistic ethic.

The acquisitive era lasted from the start of the tenth century to about the middle of the fourteenth, when some unforeseen events, such as the bubonic plague of 1348 and the Hundred Years War between England and France, brought about an acquisitive-cum-laborer age, an era of conflict between ruling acquisitors and the serfs. This was a period of unprecedented crime and near anarchy in Europe. Peasants and lords fought pitched battles, resulting in bloodshed and violence.

The acquisitive-cum-laborer age, which is usually short-lived, lasted for a hundred years, till about the middle of the fifteenth century, when in a matter of twenty-five years social revolutions broke out in France, Spain, and England. In the aftermath of these revolutions, warriors came back to power, bringing about another period of absolute rule.

The second warrior age in the West began around 1460 when Louis XI defeated rebellious nobles in France and established a centralized monarchy. In Spain this task was accomplished by Queen Isabella and Prince Ferdinand in the 1470s. In England a strong monarchy reemerged in 1485 with the accession of Henry VII, who founded the Tudor dynasty. This is how the second social cycle began in the West.

The new warrior age lasted till 1688, when a historic event in England, called the Glorious Revolution, overthrew the monarch. The intellectuals then came to power again, but this time in the guise of a prime minister who, of course, ruled only indirectly—in the name of the new king. During the early eighteenth century, the primacy of intellectuals reappeared in other areas of Europe as well. In France, following the death of Louis XIV, the kings were extremely feeble, and their imperium was actually exercised by their council of ministers. In Central Europe, then ruled by the Austrian House of Hapsburg, the power of the state chancellors overshadowed that of the emperor.

The second age of intellectuals lasted till the 1860s, when the Industrial Revolution brought capitalists to the forefront of society. Businessmen, bankers, and merchants, who possess the acquisitive mentality, then came to prominence. Acquisitors have been ruling the West ever since.

Today, Western society is passing through another acquisitive-cum-laborer age. That is why there is so much conflict between wealthy corporations and labor unions, something reminiscent of the conflict between landlords and peasants in the feudal era; that is why there is so much crime, drug and alcohol addiction, materialism, and general malaise in society today.

This state of affairs cannot last long. Social conflict in the West will continue to grow until the acquisitive mentality is eliminated as the dominant force. Society will then move into another warrior age.

3

THE LONG-RUN CYCLE OF MONEY GROWTH IN THE UNITED STATES

HISTORICAL DETERMINISM is an idea that is difficult to prove, and few today have any faith in it. That history follows a certain predictable pattern sounds incredible, because society and its institutions are subject to constant change. Yet some of the most prominent historians have been convinced that history is rhythmical, and that social events, however random they appear on the surface, follow a certain path. Were those historians mistaken, or did they see what others could not? This is indeed a complex puzzle to solve.

It is true that the early historical determinists could not provide positive proof for their hypotheses. In their times there was hardly any data, nor the institutions to collect it. Today, however, we do have the data, which extend over two to three hundred years. If historical determinism is a valid concept, then it must be supportable by the great wealth of statistics that have been collected all the way back to the eighteenth century. This is precisely what I now intend to do. Specifically, I will argue and then demonstrate that in the United States, at least, society has evolved through an acquisitive era ever since Independence. In the process, a few myths popular among economists will come to light.

WESTERN SOCIETY AND THE UNITED STATES

Before examining the empirical evidence, it is necessary to see how capitalism has evolved, especially in the United States, which is among the youngest offshoots of Western civilization. The United States is currently the nerve center of capitalism, and its history deserves a separate treatment.

In terms of Sarkar's thesis, U.S. history presents few complications. It is easy to see that from the earliest influx of Europeans to the North American continent, the United States has been moving through an acquisitive age. This is not to suggest that capitalism has always prevailed in American society, only that from the country's inception the forces of wealth have been predominant. Prior to the Civil War (1861–65), landed proprietors of great wealth were in command of society and government, but since then supremacy has passed to owners of capital and industry. Thus, in one form or another, the affluent have dominated U.S. society right from its birth.

Although it is customary to commence U.S. history from 1492, the fateful year in which Columbus discovered America, American settlements really began in 1607 when an English merchant company arrived at Jamestown and founded the colony of Virginia. Another colony was established in 1620 at Plymouth—this time by the Pilgrims, who left England to avoid persecution by James I and the Anglican Church. These two experiments were merely the beginning of what turned out to be a steady stream of immigrants sailing from Europe, especially England, to America. Within the span of a century, thirteen English colonies were established along the Atlantic coast. In addition, Spain and France occupied parts of what today is the U.S. mainland.

Europeans came to settle in the colonies for a wide variety of reasons. Some groups, such as the Puritans, Quakers, Jews, Roman Catholics, and Huguenots, came for the sake of religious freedom. Others, like the English merchants, were lured by trade and good economic prospects. Most of the early settlers were determined to assert religious and economic freedom. Having suffered much at home, they were not inclined to accept a monarchy or any other autocratic government in the colonies. They had come as private groups of people, and, except in the earliest years, they did not regard themselves as agents of the British king or of anyone else who could command them from abroad. For all these reasons, the system of government that developed in the colonies was far more representative than its British counterpart. Even as England chafed under the autocracy of the Stuart kings, the colonists enjoyed some degree of democratic government.

The basic structure of colonial governments resembled the British archetype. Each colony was headed by a governor, appointed either by the king or, as in Maryland, Delaware, and Pennsylvania, by private proprietors who, in hopes of high profits, had decided to attempt settlement in the New World. The governor was advised by an appointed council and a lower house, which was elected by those who satisfied certain property requirements. In theory, therefore, each colonial government could have been an autocracy dominated by the governor or the proprietor, but in practice the real power gradually passed to elected legislators, who were either owners of vast estates or, as in New England, wealthy merchants.

Colonial America is often pictured as a homogeneous society with few of the class conflicts that bedeviled contemporary Europe. This was perhaps true of the early settlements, but as the abundance of natural resources led to high economic growth, social stratification resulted from differing individual fortunes. The early settlers tended to have an advantage over the latecomers, as they occupied the best tracts of land. In any case, even though few aristocratic families migrated from England to the colonies, and even though most colonists brought with them little wealth, a native aristocracy, based on wealth, had developed by the eighteenth century. In America, unlike England, capital and labor were extremely scarce, but land and natural resources were abundant. In England wealth belonged to capitalists, in America to owners of vast estates, especially those in the Middle and Southern colonies. It was mainly in New England, which throve on trade and commerce, that wealthy merchants appeared, and there, unlike contemporary Europe, no stigma was attached to income derived from trade.

Regardless of the source of wealth, those who owned it commanded great esteem and influence in colonial America. A coveted office was membership on the governor's council, which was generally composed of the richest men in the land. Appointed for life, the councilmen participated in the making of laws as well as in executive decisions. Eventually, the governors and their councils were overshadowed by the elected legislative assemblies, but the assemblymen too were far from men of humble means. This sway of wealth in early American life emerges strikingly in the words of Charles A. and Mary R. Beard:

> In each colony the representative assembly, by whatever process instituted, was elected by the property owners. The qualifications imposed on voters were often modified but in every change the power of property . . . was expressly recognized. In the South, where agriculture was the great eco-

> nomic interest, land was the basis of suffrage; Virginia, for example, required the elector in town or country to be a freeholder, an owner of land—a farm or a town lot of a stated size. Where agriculture and trade divided the honors, politics reflected the fact; in Massachusetts, for instance, the suffrage was conferred upon all men who owned real estate yielding forty shillings a year income, or possessed other property to the value of £40.[10]

Thus, from its beginnings, American society has shown all the hallmarks of an acquisitive age, and although religion also played a strong role in the early settlements, its influence was soon swept aside by the rising tide of economic growth and prosperity. While the eighteenth century of Western civilization in Europe remained in the intellectuals' age, its offspring, colonial America, was already firmly in the acquisitive mode. Of course, at this time in history, America held only a minor position in the West. This was partly a matter of population. The U.S. population, though growing at astronomical rates, was for a long time just a fraction of the population of England and France. It was only after 1850 that America overtook either in this regard. Nor did the new nation have an influential voice in Western affairs; England and France remained dominant until the end of the nineteenth century. It was not until the turn of the twentieth century that the United States assumed leadership of the Western world. The Industrial Revolution had originated in England, but by the late nineteenth century America had far surpassed every European nation in industrial might. Capitalism had its roots in British soil, but it was in America that it attained its greatest triumphs, its full bloom. Thus, it was only toward the end of the nineteenth century that America began to affix its stamp on the West, and by then the leading nations of western Europe had also moved into the acquisitive age. The fact that America, even in its formative phase, had begun with an acquisitive era, while its European parents were moving through a warrior or intellectuals' age, does not in any way impair the validity of the law of social cycles for Western civilization. The United States was not then what it is today.

The thirteen American colonies, strewn along the Atlantic coast, remained under the formal dominion of Britain until a series of British policies designed to squeeze more taxes out of the colonies led to their revolt. Out of that revolutionary turmoil, the American nation was born. Though now democratic forces could make themselves felt, the supremacy of wealth continued. The new nation made a fresh start by adopting a constitution, which has served it well to this day. Three different branches of government—legislative, executive, and judicial—were established, with each serving as a check on the potential abuse of power by the other two. Within a few years, the Bill of Rights, guaranteeing certain fundamental rights to all people, not just citizens, was added to the Constitution. In this document, the acquisitor's imprint can be clearly seen. While it contained some human rights—freedom of worship, speech, the press, and petition, among others—it ignored the fundamental human right to gainful employment. Yet the unlimited right to private property was duly included.

Even though the U.S. Constitution did not establish a democracy based on universal suffrage, as voting rights still derived from property qualifications, it was nevertheless the first experiment in history to ensure a rule of law and not of men and institutions. In practice, of course, the intent of this noble document was frequently flouted, for its enforcement was still left to men, yet it was more humanitarian than any other set of principles guiding contemporary governments. True, it did not abolish slavery, but slavery had been an American institution since pre-Independence times. Ultimately, however, the Constitution did play an indirect role in its abolition. It was not without a frightful civil war (1861–65) that Abraham Lincoln could finally exorcise the curse of slavery from the nation; yet it was under the auspices of the Constitution that Lincoln, born of ordinary parentage, could in the first place become U.S. President. Thus the Constitution is a magnificent document that can take credit for many admirable achievements, but it has also been frequently abused by powerful acquisitors in American society.

One notable instance of this abuse immediately comes to mind. Until the Civil War, land and natural resources were the main factors of production. While manufacturing was far from backward, agriculture had been the dominant sector until that time. This fact, of course, had been reflected in politics, as the political arena, with but few exceptions, was a playground for landed magnates as late as the mid-nineteenth century. Following the Civil War, however, the roles were gradually reversed. Although agriculture continued to grow, it failed to keep up with manufacturing, which became the major sector of the economy. This was not a sudden development, but a product of decades of industrialization and capital accumulation. Politics reflected this gradual shift of economic power from landholders to businessmen and merchants. At the outset, there was only one political party—the Federalists—which was dominated by landed interests with no effective opposition. The birth of the modern system of two parties, each with distinctive programs, styles, and policies, was a later development which reached its culmination in 1854, when the Democratic Party, formed in 1825, was opposed by the new Republican Party. However, while the political parties differed in significant ways, they both gradually felt the increasing influence of businessmen, bankers, and merchants. Acting in their own interests, powerful business leaders attempted to turn the Constitution to their advantage.

Following the Civil War, the U.S. Congress passed the first civil rights act as the Fourteenth Amendment to the Constitution. Ostensibly, blacks were to be major beneficiaries of this law, which granted them citizenship and equal rights and forbade any state government from taking away the life, liberty, or property of any person without due process of law. However, for several decades the Fourteenth Amendment did little to protect the civil rights of blacks, who were forced to live in misery, squalor, and poverty—hardly better than slavery. Instead, the amendment became a handy tool in the hands of big business for self-enrichment. Most state courts ruled that corporations were persons and therefore entitled to protection under the due process clause. Each time a state government passed legislation to curb the antisocial practices of a corporation, federal courts would step in and proclaim the state regulation unconstitutional, contending that it flouted the due process clause of the amendment. State governments thus became helpless before the might of giant enterprises.

Unencumbered by any state intervention, and with the federal government at their service, corporations throve in America as never before. The economy grew at an unprecedented rate, while small businesses were gobbled up by a few giants. The wheeling and dealing that went on among unscrupulous businessmen toward the end of the nineteenth century earned them the label "robber barons," men who, according to Gilbert Fite and Jim Reese, "built poor railroads, turned out shoddy products, cheated honest investors, sweated labor, and exploited the country's natural resources for their own wealth and satisfaction."[11] Almost every major industry became a monopoly. The economy might not have grown as fast without them, but there were certainly distressing side effects of this concentration of economic power on so vast a scale—a malady that U.S. society has never since been able to shake off. So outrageous were monopolistic business practices that by 1889 the whole country was up in arms. In response, Congress passed the Sherman Antitrust Act, which barred any person or corporation from conspiring to form monopolies or to stifle competition in any way. This, however, turned out to be a carrot dangled by the business-dominated Congress before an aroused public. As with the Fourteenth Amendment, this act too was eventually used by corporations to their own advantage.

For the next few decades, the Sherman Act was interpreted by the courts in a way that emasculated labor unions. Strikes were ruled as anticompetitive practices. Thus a law meant to protect the public eventually became an antilabor law.

What producers detest most is competition among themselves, for competition increases uncertainty and trims profits. Toward the end of the nineteenth century, while most industries became concentrated in the hands of a few owners, railroads continued to be competitive. In fact, the competition was so intense that the owners themselves demanded regulation from Congress, which, of course, was quick to oblige them. In 1887 Congress established the Interstate Commerce Commission (ICC) to regulate the railroads in the public interest. Thus, one might say that from the Civil War down to the fateful year of 1929, the first year of the Great Depression, the acquisitive era was in its upswing. Big business flourished on all fronts. On the one hand, feeble antitrust laws like the Sherman Act provided the smokescreen under which monopolies, oligopolies, and trusts could flourish while labor unions remained on the leash; on the other, various regulatory commissions such as the ICC were instituted to eliminate cutthroat competition among oligopolies, enabling them to cooperate for their survival. In one industry after another, competition, the most powerful restraint on exuberant profits, was smothered.

That capitalism is subject to unique internal traumas is the conventional wisdom in modern economics, and the symptoms of this malady were discernible as early as the birth of the Republic. U.S. capitalism was in its infancy when it had its first bout with economic depression in 1782; it weathered that storm, only to be hit by it again and again. In all, during the first half of the nineteenth century it suffered four economic crises; during the second half it experienced five (in 1854, 1857, 1873, 1884, and 1893). The twentieth century opened with brighter prospects, but the specter of depression still hung over the economy. After giving a mild foretaste of its impending assault in 1907, 1921, and 1927, it struck with a vengeance on October 24, 1929—the day of the Great Crash. On that day, the bottom fell out of the New York Stock Exchange. The downward spiral of security prices that then began quickly engulfed the American economy, and eventually the entire capitalist world. Within three years, the economic catastrophe of the Great Depression had caused 85,000 business failures in America, and 12 million people, equal to 25 percent of the labor force, were unemployed.

The economic blight spread overnight to other troubled nations linked with the American economy through international commerce. The entire Western world stood on the verge of collapse. The apocalyptic Marxist vision of the demise of capitalism seemed at hand. But then came a brilliant economist, John Maynard Keynes, and the Second World War. Keynes prescribed the medicine, and the war served to show that it could work. Under the enormous government expenditures occasioned by the war, unemployment slowly disappeared and, for a while, gave way to labor shortages. Keynes had recommended massive doses of government spending to combat unemployment, and the war proved him right. Ever since, Keynesian economic theory and its offshoots have been largely guiding the Western world.

Under the watchful eyes of Keynesian policymakers, capitalism seemed to be operating smoothly for a full quarter of a century following the Second World War. There were mild relapses occasionally, but no duplication of the 1929 tragedy. But just when the war against economic crises seemed to have been won, another intractable problem, potentially more dangerous than large-scale unemployment, cropped up and has persisted since 1969—namely, the coexistence of inflation with a high level of unemployment. This problem eluded Keynes, for there is supposed to be a trade-off between unemployment and inflation in the Keynesian system: both cannot rise or decline at the same time. As yet there is no consensus among economists—there hardly ever is—as to how the new challenge should be met. The problem admits of no simple, and politically feasible, solution.

On top of these troubles, in 1973 the world economy was jolted by an international cartel called the Organization of Petroleum Exporting Countries (OPEC). There was a fourfold rise in oil prices as a result, and the U.S. economy tottered once again. The recession of 1973–75 was the steepest since the Great Crash, but more than that, it was accompanied by unprecedented double-digit inflation. Keynesian remedies were applied once again, and as a consequence the economy recovered, only to be hit by another bout of stagflation lasting from 1980 to 1982. Since then, both inflation and unemployment have declined, but, as no fundamental reform has been undertaken, the crisis is still simmering, ready to erupt again at any moment.

In the 1980s, the United States has been passing through an acquisitive-cum-laborer age, which appears toward the end of the supremacy of acquisitors. In fact, America moved into this era at the turn of the 1970s when President Richard Nixon and Vice President Spiro Agnew were driven out of office because of their unscrupulous activities. Agnew was forced to resign in 1973 after pleading no contest in federal court to charges of income tax evasion and bribery. A year later Nixon, who was bloodied in the Watergate scandal, preferred to quit rather than face certain impeachment by the Senate.

These shocking events were unprecedented in U.S. history. Not one but both heads of state had disgraced themselves and their nation. This is precisely the kind of lawlessness in government that marks the acquisitive-cum-laborer age, where the dominant class increasingly turns to illegal activities in its pursuit of wealth and power. The general effect is to weaken the moral fiber of the nation, for the public consciously or unconsciously tends to follow its leaders and the result is a steep jump in crime, dishonesty, and greed in society.

Evidently the abuse of administrative power did not end with the Nixon-Agnew resignations, and at the federal, state, and local levels a seemingly unending chain of unethical and illegal activities by government officials has since come to light. In both the Carter and Reagan administrations there have been highly publicized examples of the misuse of power. Corruption at the local level in our larger cities now seems almost endemic.

With America currently in the grip of the acquisitive-cum-laborer age, it is not surprising to see a rising tide of crime, drug and alcohol addiction, family breakdown, a high rate of divorce, child abuse, increasing poverty for the poor and the middle class, greater disparity in income and wealth, and massive economic hemorrhage brought about by enormous trade and budget deficits. If there is a silver lining to all this, it is that such a tragic situation cannot last: it will force a crisis that will ultimately give way to sanity in politics, the economy, and the general state of affairs.

Theories Underlying Capitalism

No socioeconomic system can last long unless it rests on an appealing ideological structure. In this regard, capitalism is no exception. And, as with every elitist system, its ideological thread is sound in theory but tenuous in reality.

Capitalism is defined as a social, economic, and political system where the means of production—industries, banks, natural resources, etc.—are owned by private corporations and individuals, where the political system operates in the interests of such owners, and where the distribution of national income is determined by them. It is closely associated with the free enterprise system, which may be defined as one where businessmen, the owners of the means of production, are free to maximize their profits.

We have already seen that in an acquisitive era intellectuals come forward to offer theories justifying the supremacy of the acquisitors. To many intellectuals, it seems to matter little how specious their justification is as long as it serves their purpose. Only a few advocate genuine reform and concern for the exploited, much to the dislike of those in power. It is in this broad perspective that the economic theory of capitalism propounded by Adam Smith, the father of economics, ought to be viewed. The period between 1500 and 1700 is traditionally associated with mercantilism, which to some extent overlapped with the preceding warrior age. It was during this period that the foundation for modern-day capitalism was laid, despite state regulations curbing the activities of merchants and industrialists. The real driving force behind capitalism—the acquisitive instinct or the profit motive—was sanctioned neither by the state nor the church. Since the church had submitted to the king, the responsibility for restraining the merchants from unbridled pursuit of self-interest fell to the crown. However, state regulations continued to derive from medieval ideology—the Christian paternalistic ethic.

Following the Glorious Revolution of 1688, dogmas exalting the power of the state gave way to those exalting individualism and ultimately the acquisitive instinct. All this ferment occurred during an era in which income from land commanded more prestige than profits from trade. Thus when Adam Smith wrote his masterpiece, *The Wealth of Nations,* in 1776, the merchant class, though not as encumbered by state regulations as during the preceding warrior era, was still not completely free to pursue its quest for profits. Smith's argument was that human beings are moved primarily by selfish and egoistic motives; that all human actions are rooted in self-preservation, and hence self-interest and ambition are not vices but virtues, leading to hard work and economic prosperity. By implication, then, the state should keep its intervention in economic activities to a minimum so that individual and social welfare is at the maximum.

This sanction of acquisitive behavior that had found support from the intellectuals—many of whom were employed by the great trading enterprises—was readily embraced by the business interests. But its excessive stress on individualism produced apprehensions of anarchy in many minds. It was Smith's brilliant contribution that tended to calm their fears. His carefully thought out analysis of the capitalist system, based on keen competition, removed from the doctrine of individualism many of its flaws that had worked to impede its general acceptance.

Smith argued that, left to themselves, producers and workers are guided by self-interest to put their capital and labor to uses where they are the most productive. The mechanism that ensures this is the "invisible hand" of a free market, where businessmen compete for consumers' money in an egocentric search for profits, and where consumers seek to obtain the best-quality product at the cheapest price. In quest of profit maximization, the producers are impelled to produce only those goods for which there is demand and to use the most efficient techniques so that unit costs are minimized. In a free-market economy, therefore, everyone is happy: the producers earn maximum returns, and consumers are satisfied with high-quality products available at the lowest prices ensured by maximum productive efficiency. All this is the miracle performed by the "invisible hand" in spite of, or rather because of, human greed and acquisitive behavior.

Smith assailed the myriad mercantilist regulations that had

worked to perpetuate monopolies, for monopolies destroy operation of the free market that ensures maximum social welfare. His work, therefore, was on the one hand a scathing denunciation of mercantilism and on the other an eloquent plea for free enterprise, or laissez-faire. However, the free enterprise system that Smith had in mind condoned the producer's search for profit, but only in an environment characterized by competition.

The doctrine of laissez-faire, first propounded by Adam Smith and later refined by his disciples such as David Ricardo and J. B. Say, is now known as the classical theory of economics. With this economic ideology went a political creed that considered the state as a necessary evil—evil because of its encroachments on individual liberty, but necessary as a bulwark against anarchy.

At the time Smith wrote his book, capitalism was still in its infancy. His vision of a competitive system where the consumer is sovereign and the powerless producer is scrambling to satisfy market demand did, to an extent, reflect economic reality. But by the late nineteenth century, capitalism had grown into adolescence. Throughout the West, especially in Germany and America, industrial giants had sprung up to undermine the market mechanism that is supposed to generate maximum social welfare. While the forces of demand were free to operate, those of supply had been effectively constrained. But all this failed to deter a new breed of economists from erecting an even nobler defense of the free enterprise system.

At precisely the time when the process of industrial concentration was under way, some economists, notably Jevons, Walras, and Marshall among others, set out to clothe the classical economic ideology with an elaborate mathematical apparatus, while maintaining the assumption of perfect competition. Theirs is the so-called neoclassical economic analysis, but in their basic theme of espousing laissez-faire they differ little from their precursors. Thus, while the assumptions underlying capitalism had been drastically altered, economic theory emerged with new makeup applied to the old face. Even as the robber barons were storing away national wealth in their coffers, the neoclassical economists recommended "hands off" economic policies by the government, lest the giant corporations be inhibited from acting in the public interest.

The neoclassical economists thus raised the "invisible hand" mechanism of Adam Smith to an even higher pedestal and added their own voices to the growing mystique of laissez-faire, while choosing to be blind to surrounding economic reality. While the reality clamored for an end to the bulging concentration of power, to monopolies and trusts, to the staggering corruption in the business arena, the economists confined themselves to their idealized conception of the world. As a result, economic theory was ill-prepared to prescribe a remedy for any economic cataclysm such as the one that beset the world in 1929. The neoclassical economists had undying faith in the ability of capitalism to pull itself out of any crisis as long as the state abstained from interfering. In their view, official intervention could only make matters worse.

The Great Crash of 1929, therefore, caught economists napping in their idealized world. The ensuing depression would not last long, they assured the public; market forces would reassert themselves and set things aright. The entire Western world was then engulfed not by any natural calamity, not by any war on which the public wrath could be easily focused, but by a man-made calamity with no escape in sight. Before the remedy could be prescribed, the malady had to be properly diagnosed; venerated dogmas had to be discarded.

It was Keynes who set out to reshape and fundamentally reorganize economic theory to bring it in line with reality. In contrast to the major neoclassical concern with microeconomics, i.e., the economic behavior of individual economic units such as businessmen, consumers, etc., he addressed himself to the question of macro-economics, i.e., the analysis of the entire economy. Keynes observed that businesses perform a two-pronged function: as producers they supply goods, but they also pay incomes to households in the form of wages, rents, interest, and profits. The households in turn spend money to buy goods from businessmen. There is thus a circular flow, with income flowing from producers to consumers and then from consumers back to producers. As long as businessmen can sell all their goods at a reasonable profit, this circular process continues uninterrupted.

But several hitches may arise. A part of an individual's income is saved and deposited with financial institutions, a part taken away by the government in the form of taxes, and a part spent on foreign goods in the form of imports. These are what we may call leakages from total expenditure, and they tend to keep aggregate demand for goods short of the aggregate supply. Counterbalancing these leakages are the three injections to total expenditure—business borrowing for investment, government spending, and exports. If the leakages are matched by injections, total spending matches the total value of goods produced, and the economy may be said to be in equilibrium, that is, it has no tendency to move up or down. If the leakages exceed injections, aggregate demand falls short of aggregate supply and some goods remain unsold, so that businessmen are forced to trim production and hence their employment of labor; in the opposite case of the injections exceeding leakages, production and hence employment tend to rise.

This, in simple terms, is the well-known Keynesian process of national income determination. In this system aggregate demand plays an active role, and aggregate supply a passive role in the sense that the latter converges to the former. High national income and hence high employment call for high aggregate demand. The corollary is unmistakably clear: during years of low demand, the economy suffers from high unemployment and hence recessions or depressions. The policy prescription is also unmistakably clear: in order to cure unemployment, the government should step in and raise aggregate spending in the economy by means of fiscal and monetary policies.

Fiscal policy involves the weighing of government expenditure versus tax receipts. During a depression, fiscal policy calls for a budget deficit, i.e., for government expenditure to exceed tax revenue; but with inflation, the cure lies in a budget surplus. Monetary policy, by contrast, affects the economy indirectly—through its effect on business investment. Keynes argued that monetary expansion encourages investment, while a contraction discourages it. Hence during a depression, the monetary policy has to be expansionary, but during inflation, contractional.

Keynesian economics is thus the antithesis of the neoclassical ideology, for the government is now cast in the role of a constant watchdog indispensable to continued prosperity. The appeal of Keynesian theory lay in the fact that not only did it properly diagnose the economic ills, but it also advocated policies well within the reach of governments. For this reason its spread was swift and decisive, despite stubborn initial resistance from doctrinaire economists who detested any state intervention on purely ideological grounds. Today Keynesian thought has become the orthodoxy to which challenges from other quarters are often posed. The most notable challenge was mounted in the 1960s by Nobel laureate Milton Friedman, who is credited with pioneering a whole new approach, called the monetarist approach, to the question of economic fluctuations under capitalism.

In a way, what Friedman has done is to partially rehabilitate the neoclassical economic theory. He may be regarded as the Adam Smith of the twentieth century, for he too has championed the philosophy of laissez-faire in the midst of an economic environment that has swerved away from it.

Friedman argues that the source of most economic cycles is the monetary sector and not, as Keynes believed, the goods (or investment) sector; that is, the single most important determinant of price levels and employment rates is the level of money supply. While to Keynes the deficiency of investment relative to savings is the catalyst for recessions, to Friedman the causal factor is the change in the community's stock of money, whose growth, he argues, had shrunk prior to the advent of any recession in the United States. Furthermore, this shrinkage was in most cases brought about either by inept actions of monetary authorities or by the intrusion of politicians. Unlike Keynes, therefore, he does not believe that it is possible to fine-tune the economy and still expect it to remain in good health. Government, to him, ought to be limited mainly to protecting property rights, printing money, administering the judicial system, and maintaining law and order. Thus, monetarism differs fundamentally from Keynesian economics, which argues that the economy is basically unstable and that the main source of instability is the level of investment. To stabilize the system, therefore, the government should actively intervene in the economy by following appropriate fiscal and monetary policies.

Monetarists, by contrast, argue that the economy is basically stable and that government intervention does not help or, at worst, may itself be the cause of instability. The government, in their view, ought to restrain itself by balancing its budget over the business cycle and by permitting monetary expansion at the annual rate of 4 percent or whatever is the long-run rate of growth of output. This is because when money and output grow at the same rate, inflation becomes zero. Implicit here is the belief that government can control the supply of money, which to Monetarists is the most important determinant of economic activity.

Current economic thought reflects what can only be called a massive state of confusion, of which a prime example is the so-called supply-side economics. Also known as Reaganomics, this creed gained popularity with Reagan's election as President in 1980. Reaganomics is really a distorted replica of classical economics—distorted because, while it seeks to trim the size of the government, it is, at best, indifferent to the classical prescription of balancing the budget. The supply-siders argue that instead of raising aggregate demand the government should help the private sector increase its supply of goods and services. The government can best assist by cutting taxes for individuals and businesses and by reducing unproductive federal regulations in the areas of pollution control, affirmative action, etc. All this would create so much economic growth that eventually tax revenues would rise even with lower tax rates.

In 1981 Congress approved much of Reagan's economic program, which resulted in a massive tax cut, mostly for affluent individuals and large corporations. However, federal spending was hardly touched, as cuts in social programs were matched by large increases in defense spending. Reagan won enactment of his program by pledging that by 1984 it would balance the federal budget, which had been in arrears by as much as $60 billion under his Democratic predecessor, Jimmy Carter.

Reagan's remedies were the standard Keynesian prescriptions, which called for reduced taxes to cure a recession besetting the economy in 1980 and 1981. Such policies almost invariably deepen the budget deficit. Apparently, by labeling his tax cuts "supply-side cuts," Reagan thought he was going to defy the conventional wisdom and produce a balanced budget by 1984. It is as if semantics and rhetoric were going to generate an economic miracle and frustrate the laws of mathematics.

The inevitable happened. By 1983 the federal deficit exceeded $200 billion. In fact, the debt accumulated during Reagan's first term alone dwarfed the total indebtedness incurred from the very beginning of the Republic. In response, Congress passed the Gramm-Rudman Deficit Reduction Act of 1985, which required a balanced budget by 1991. Whether this bill will actually eliminate or even trim the deficit remains to be seen, because for fiscal year 1986 the deficit reached a new high of $220 billion.

Supply-side economics is indicative of the massive confusion that exists in economic theory today. It is really the failed policy of Keynesian economics in a new bottle, and even though the packaging is new, the results are likely to be old—short-term prosperity to be followed by long-term blight. Reaganomics, as I shall argue in Chapter 7, is likely to lead to another depression. However, confusion is exactly what one can expect from the acquisitive-cum-laborer age.

MONETARISM AND THE SOCIAL CYCLE

Let us now see what Sarkar's position is in this connection. According to his law of social cycles, capitalism is synonymous with the West's second age of acquisitors and it is they who control the levers of not only the economy but of everything else in society.

To Sarkar, every entity, animate or inanimate, evolves in a cyclical fashion. Though within each era the ruling class itself is subject to ups and downs, it remains dominant, and its preeminence determines the cycle of all other variables. The dominant class is the nucleus of society, and around the cyclical fortunes of this nucleus revolve all social phenomena. During the acquisitive era, the power and prestige of the class atop the social hierarchy derive from its control and ownership of wealth. Under capitalism, for instance, the wealthy are supreme because they own a large proportion of the means of production.

In the current age of acquisitors, the fortunes of businessmen, the dominant class, are associated with the supply of money. Under capitalism, money and wealth are closely related: they are almost synonymous. Since the wealthy are currently on top, and since money and wealth move together, under capitalism the supply of money must be the most important determinant of all social variables, including the economy. This is simply an echo of Friedman's position, *but why money is the primary determinant of economic activity under capitalism can be adequately explained only by Sarkar's law of social cycles.*

How can we prove this proposition? How can the doubts raised by Keynesians and other skeptics be resolved? In support of his view, Friedman cites the postwar behavior of the American economy, where annual fluctuations in the growth of both money and gross national product have declined. Keynesians, however, have countered by arguing that, first, the money growth is hard to control, and second, the change in GNP may be generating the change in money supply and not vice versa, so that money need not hold the pivotal position in the economy.

There is only one way to demonstrate decisively that money, nothing else, is the source of all oscillations under capitalism. And that is to pose the most difficult test. Since every entity is cyclical, the dominant entity also has a cycle. But this cycle must be rhythmical. This is because the primary variable must have an exact and stable cycle of its own. How else could it regulate the cycles of others? How else could it be dominant?

Thus, the test that we have posed is this. If money is the primary variable in society, its growth must follow a cyclical path of constant pattern or rhythm. Stated differently, unless the economy is in a complete shambles, the cycle of money growth must hit either a peak or a trough every *x* number of years.

There can be no criterion tougher than this. Cycles of varying durations, mentioned in Chapter 1, have been discovered for many variables in the past, but none displays the exactness demanded by the test posed above. If any such cycle exists, then it is proof not only of the supreme position of that variable in society, but also of the broader concept of historical determinism underlying the law of social cycles. Note that our concern here is not with the time path of money supply but with its growth. This is because we are analyzing an economy that has been growing over time.

THE CYCLE OF MONEY GROWTH

Let us now examine the empirical evidence. From the data sources described in the Appendix to Chapter 3, one can obtain consistent estimates of money supply going as far back as the birth of the American nation in 1776. These figures, in the words of Milton Friedman and Anna Schwartz, "fragile as they may be, show no obvious discontinuity with the money stock estimates for the century after 1867."[12] True, a little conjecture is involved in estimating money supply prior to 1800, but following that year reliable figures are available, and the series constructed by John Gurley and Edward Shaw comes very close to the methodology used by Friedman and Schwartz in obtaining statistics for later years.[13] A simple transformation of these observations into rates of change per decade yields a vivid cycle, presented in Chart 1. Here the decennial rate of money growth is the percentage change per decade in the supply of money, specifically Old M2, which is defined as currency in the hands of the public plus demand and time deposits with commercial banks.

Chart 1 / **The Long-Run Cycle of Money Growth per Decade in the United States (1770s–1970s)**

Except for the aftermath of the Civil War in the 1860s, the money-growth rate per decade reached its peak every third decade over more than two centuries.

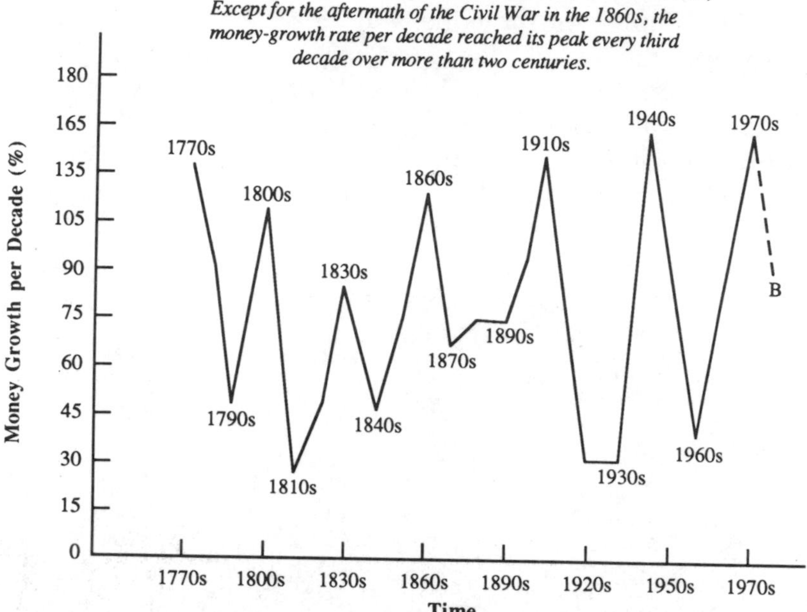

Sources: Friedman and Schwartz, and Ravi Batra; see Appendix to Chapter 3.

The money-growth cycle in Chart 1 begins with the 1770s, for no figures of any kind are available on money supply prior to that decade. The 1770s, being the decade of the American Revolution, experienced extraordinary money growth. Historians argue that money growth during the 1770s was greater than at any time in colonial America.

Chart 1 reveals that the decennial rate of money growth has followed a long-term cycle, reaching a peak every third decade, with the singular exception of the two decades following the Civil War of the 1860s.

Immediately after the Civil War, regarded as the most cataclysmic event in U.S. history, the money-growth cycle was disrupted. The economy took about twenty years to recuperate, but once the recovery was complete by the 1880s, the cycle resumed its rhythmical course, because within the next three decades money growth crested in the 1910s, which is the first peak decade of the twentieth century. Thirty years later, the money-growth peak recurs in the 1940s, and then again in the 1970s. If we were to plot on Chart 1, the money-growth rate between 1980 and 1986 and if that rate were to continue through the 1980s, we could obtain a point such as *B*, indicating that the 1970s were unmistakably the most recent peak of the cycle. Money growth in the 1980s has declined, though not by much.

Thus Chart 1 shows that, except for the post–Civil War period, the decennial rate of money growth crested every third decade over the past two centuries. This is an amazing feature of the U.S. economy, and it fits deftly with Sarkar's hypothesis that the dominant variable of any age follows a rhythmical cycle.

Why was the cycle disrupted in the aftermath of the Civil War? The reason is that the war left the U.S. economy in a shambles. While every entity, according to Sarkar, follows a cyclical movement, its normal pattern is disturbed if it suffers a major external shock. It may then become comatose for a while; but after it recovers, it begins its normal cyclical pattern once again. What is important here is to remember that the period of recuperation is followed by the same old rhythm, unless, of course, the entity dies.

This is precisely how the U.S. economy behaved after the Civil War, which, lasting from 1861 to 1865, shook the very foundations of American society. While the South was devastated, the North suffered heavy damage from the loss of capital and skilled labor. Never before, nor since, has the American nation been so traumatized. Even the two world wars did not cause so much havoc and destruction, because they were fought on foreign soil.

It took the U.S. economy about two decades to recover from the Civil War, because from the 1880s onward the decennial rate of money growth resumed its cycle, reaching another peak in thirty years, in the 1910s. The three-decade cycle has continued ever since. In the discussion that follows, we will ignore in our analysis the disruption of the money-growth cycle in the aftermath of the Civil War, assuming that such an event is not likely to recur in the near future.

Historical Determinism

What are the implications of the long-term cycle of money growth displayed in Chart 1? First, money supply or wealth is the nucleus around which every entity in American society, not just the economy, revolves, and has done so at least since Independence. This implies that the United States has been in the age of acquisitors all this time.

Second, the cycle vividly illustrates the concept of historical determinism which has so often been ridiculed and reviled. That history follows a definite pattern can no longer be in dispute. Economists of all persuasions agree that the money supply is influenced by a large spectrum of forces seemingly unrelated to each other. How could they all converge to follow a set path spanning more than two centuries? It is as if there were a principle of nature that brings order to the apparently disorderly currents of society, a natural law that dictates that the time has now come for money growth to soar, now to stabilize, now to fall.

We'll find further support for the concept of historical determinism in the next two chapters, which reveal that the long-run decennial cycle of the type exhibited in Chart 1 also exists for at least two other variables, namely the rate of inflation and the degree of economic regulation by the government. Thus the money-growth cycle is no fluke, but has ample company.

Third, the Keynesians are correct in their claim that the money supply cannot be controlled by authorities. Friedman argues for a fixed money-growth rule to be followed by the Federal Reserve System. Most economists attribute the decline of money growth in the 1980s to Paul Volcker, the Federal Reserve chief appointed in 1979, who restrained the engine of money supply in order to control inflation. However, the cycle of money growth would seem to show Volcker as merely an instrument in the hands of an invisible force, much like Adam Smith's invisible hand, guiding the destiny of the American economy; Volcker was simply the vehicle for the expression of its will. With the 1940s being the peak decade of money growth, the 1970s were destined to be the next peak decade of the three-decade cycle, and thus the 1980s were destined to experience a contraction in the growth of money. For a peak must obviously be followed by a decline.

What, then, is this invisible force? It is, according to Sarkar, the law of social cycles, which in turn is one facet of the generic principle of evolution.

The Federal Reserve System constitutes a milestone in the banking annals of the United States. It was established in 1914 for the purpose of remedying a number of weaknesses that had plagued the economy since the founding of the Republic. Prior to the Fed, money supply responded only to conditions in the money market. One would think that the creation of the Fed would have at least tamed, if not eliminated, the money-growth cycle. Instead, it had just the opposite effect. Chart 1 reveals that the amplitude of fluctuations in the decennial rate of money growth was lower during the nineteenth century than during the twentieth. Thus the creation of the Fed simply increased the long-run oscillations in money supply without in any way disrupting the pattern of the cycle.

Yet it is true that fluctuations in annual growth of money have declined since the 1940s. This suggests that the Fed can leash the money supply in the short run but not in the long run. In other words, man can control his destiny at a point of time but ultimately has to operate within certain bounds set by larger forces—bounds which cannot be defied forever.

Finally, the money-growth cycle implies that capitalism is fundamentally unstable and that the creation of institutions such as the Fed cannot stabilize it. They are mere palliatives that in the long run actually destabilize the system. What is needed is not a perfunctory cure, but fundamental economic reforms, which we shall discuss in Chapter 9.

Does all this imply that events are predetermined and that we have to be their helpless victims? Not really! All it means is that things move in terms of predictable cycles which keep occurring time after time until their true cause is discovered. Once we know their cause, we can stop them. After all, humanity has broken disastrous cycles in the past and will do so in the future as well. This is how all evolution occurs. We keep enduring recurring problems of one sort or another, until they become intolerable; then someone discovers their true cause and helps us break the cycle. Afterward, a new cycle takes over.

However, in view of the longevity of the patterns described in this work, it is clear that disrupting them will not be easy. Nothing short of fundamental reforms will work.

4

THE LONG-RUN CYCLE OF INFLATION IN THE UNITED STATES

MOST ECONOMISTS now recognize that the money supply has a major influence on many variables in the economy. While not all agree with Friedman's claim that money is the primary determinant of business activity, there is no doubt that variations in money supply and money growth accompany economic fluctuations. In the past, inordinate monetary expansion over a long period inevitably generated inflation, whereas shrinkage in the money supply was at the least associated with depressions and, according to some, might even have been their cause.

Before we can examine what causes a depression, we have to investigate the phenomenon of inflation, because in history great inflations have usually preceded great depressions. The fact that money growth in America has followed an exact cycle cresting every third decade implies that money is indeed the nucleus of capitalist society, for only a predominant entity could have such an inexorable and stable cyclical path. An analysis of the long-run trend of inflation supports this view. Specifically, we shall show that the decennial rate of inflation in the United States has also followed a cyclical path, one that precisely parallels the long-run cycle of money growth. In other words, the rate of inflation per decade has also crested every third decade for over two centuries, except during the aftermath of the Civil War. This conclusion should not, of course, come as a surprise to monetarists, who picture a close association between money growth and inflation.

Developing the Long-Run Cycle of Inflation

Inflation is generally defined as a state of persistent increase in general prices. A one-time rise in prices is not enough for the situation to be called inflationary. Unlike the cycle of money growth, the cycle of inflation is not self-evident; an averaging procedure using the data on product prices is needed to obtain it.

Let us take a close look at the annual wholesale price index (WPI) in Chart 2. (The underlying data for the chart are presented in the Appendix to Chapter 4.) There was not much change in wholesale prices from 1749 to 1939. Prices rose rapidly at times, but over the 190 years they always came down shortly after reaching their peak. Since 1939, however, prices have moved in only one direction—upward. The chart can thus be segmented into two parts: one where prices move up and down, and the other where they rise and hardly ever decline. The chart tends to mask the continuity of U.S. inflation, as it appears that a discontinuity occurs around 1939. Until then the economy seems to have experienced regular cycles of inflation, with prices reaching their peak around 1780, 1810, 1865, and 1920 and then declining precipitously

Chart 2 / **The Wholesale Price Index (WPI) in the United States (1749–1982) 1910–14=100**

The chart shows that there was not much change in the WPI in the U.S. from 1749 to 1939. Since then prices have been constantly rising, and a discontinuity in their behavior has emerged.

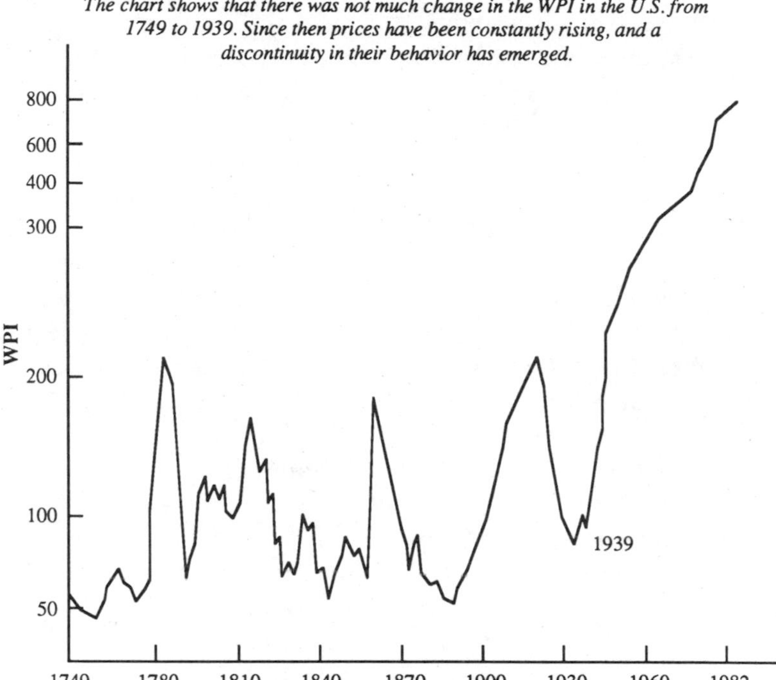

Sources: *Historical Statistics of the United States* and *Economic Report of the President;* see Appendix to Chapter 4.

every time. Even so, the chart reveals the rudiments of a long-run inflationary cycle, at least in the eighteenth and nineteenth centuries.

Let us now transform the annual data of Chart 2 into decennial data. This is a common practice among economic historians who seek to identify trends underlying the long period of any time series. To do this, we can either add up annual prices to obtain the aggregate price level in each decade or take an arithmetic mean of prices per decade to obtain the average price level. Either statistic may represent the price level per decade. Here we are working with an average of the price level, but both procedures lead to exactly the same results, because the average can be obtained by simply dividing the aggregate by 11, which is taken as the number of years in a decade, if we include the first year and the last.

Thus Chart 3 presents the average wholesale price level per decade and plots it against time. The first observation in the chart is the price level of 1749, which is assumed to represent the average price level of the 1740s.[14]

Chart 3 shows that the average price level per decade reached periodic peaks in the 1780s, 1810s, 1860s, and 1920s and then declined for some time. This chart furnishes a somewhat better picture of the inflationary cycle than Chart 2, as annual price variations have been averaged out, yet the discontinuity in the price behavior remains. Here, following the decade of the 1930s, the average price level, unlike the case in preceding decades, rises continuously and never comes down. Thus, although the cycle of inflation is now relatively well defined, it preserves the discontinuity observed in Chart 2.

But this discontinuity is more apparent than real. Let us transform the data of Chart 3 into rates of price change or inflation, and then plot them in Chart 4. There, the long-run cycle of inflation emerges as an eloquent testimony to the resilience of the American economy. It is displayed by light and thin lines moving up and down through twenty-three decades, beginning with the 1750s. Gone is the discontinuity of price behavior observed in the earlier charts. Instead, as with the money-growth cycle we traced in the previous chapter, a discontinuity appears following the 1860s—the decade of the Civil War.

Except for the post–Civil War period, Chart 4 displays an amazing phenomenon, namely that over the last 230 years the decennial rate of inflation reached a peak every third decade and then usually declined over the next two. Here the decennial

Chart 3 / **Decennial Average Wholesale Price Level with Origin at 1749 (1750–1980) 1910–14=100**

The decennial average WPI peaked during the 1780s, 1810s, 1860s, and 1920s and declined each time. Since the 1930s, it has never declined, revealing a discontinuity in the price behavior.

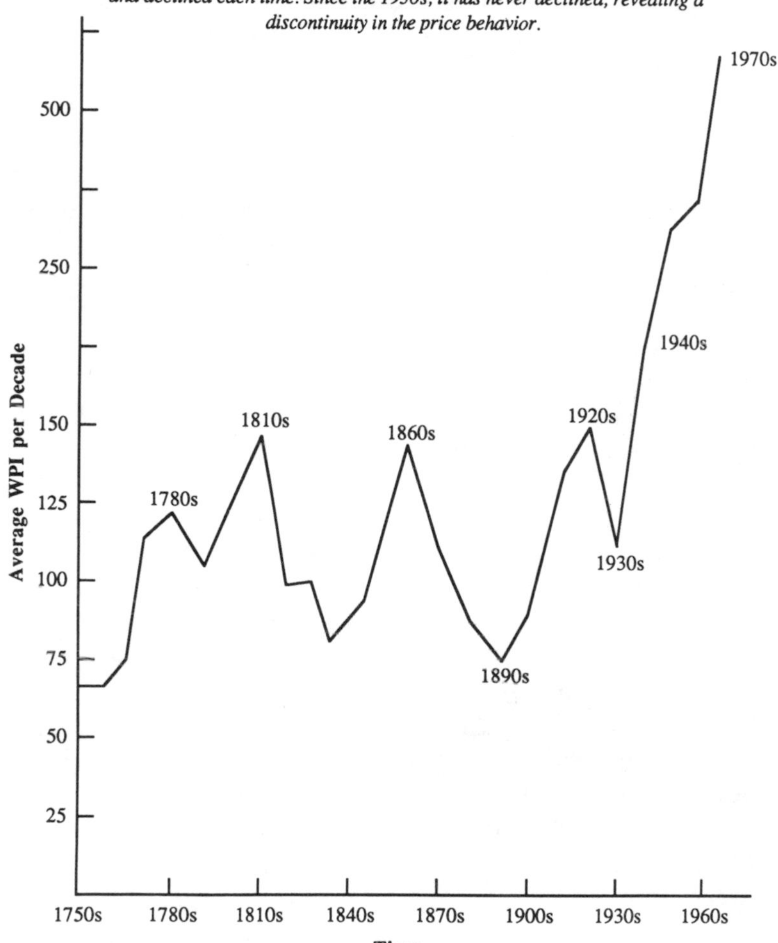

Source: *Historical Statistics of the United States;* see Appendix to Chapter 4.

rate of inflation is obtained by computing the percentage increase in average wholesale prices in each decade.

Another method is to define inflation by the proportionate change in prices within a decade, i.e., the decennial inflation rate could be obtained by dividing the difference between prices at the end and the beginning of a decade by the beginning price. If prices were always rising, this perhaps would not be an improper procedure. But, as we have seen, for the major part of U.S. economic history, prices rose and fell within a decade, and also from decade to decade, in which case the difference between prices at the end and the start of a decade could be highly misleading in that it might show price stability, whereas the average price level had in fact sharply risen above that in the previous decade. The procedure followed here not only uses all the data available for prices, but also applies to both cases—where prices rise and fall, and where they rise but do not fall.

In Chart 4 the first inflationary peak appears in the 1770s, following which the inflation rate declines over the next two decades and reaches another peak in the 1800s. Again it falls over the two subsequent decades, rising to its zenith in the 1830s. This time the inflation rate declines for only one decade, but still the next peak appears thirty years later in the 1860s. At this point the decennial cycle is disturbed, but it begins anew with the 1880s, because within three decades the peak reappears in the 1910s, which is the first inflationary peak of the twentieth century. Thirty years later the cycle crests in the 1940s, and then again thirty years later in the 1970s. If we were to plot on Chart 4 the inflation rates between 1980 and 1986, and if such rates were to continue through the 1980s, we would obtain a point such as *A,* showing that the 1970s were unmistakably the most recent peak of the decennial cycle of inflation.

The inflationary peak of the 1830s might appear curious, for it occurs virtually on the zero line. But the decades imme-

Chart 4 / **The Long-Run Cycle of Inflation in the United States (1750s–1970s)**

Except for the aftermath of the Civil War of the 1860s, the inflation rate per decade reached its peak every third decade over more than two centuries.

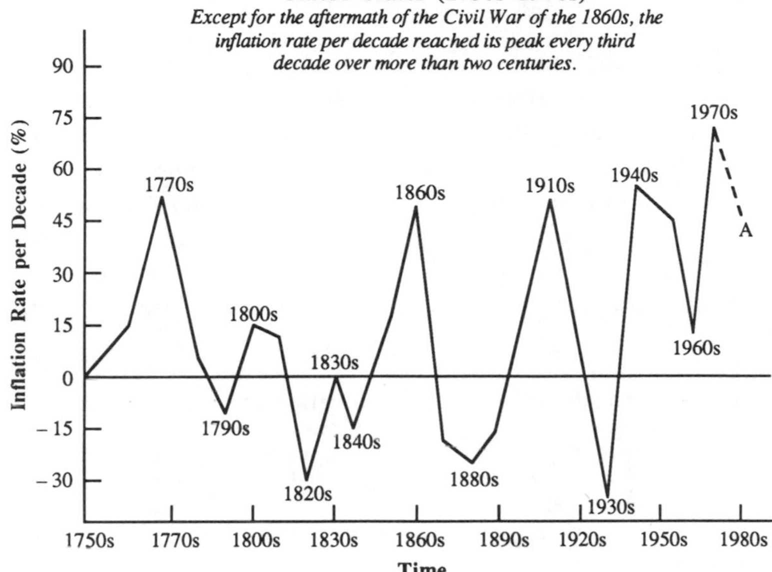

Source: See Appendix to Chapter 3.

diately preceding and following the 1830s reveal negative rates of inflation. Hence, compared to these deflationary years, the zero rate of inflation represents at least relative inflation though not inflation in the absolute sense. Thus, it is not improper to regard the 1830s as the peak of the inflation (or deflation) cycle of the three decades between 1820 and 1850. Perhaps a safer statement regarding the cycle during the nineteenth century is that the inflation peak following each trough occurred every third decade, excepting, of course, the two decades following the Civil War. Here the troughs of the cycle occur in the 1790s, 1820s, 1840s, 1880s, 1930s, and 1960s, and except in the aftermath of the Civil War, each peak following the trough appears at an interval of thirty years.

Inflation and Money Supply

What is the main cause of inflation? A great debate over this question occurred in the 1970s, but now a consensus has emerged among economists, who believe that inflation springs chiefly from prolonged monetary expansion. There may be other contributory factors, but they cannot sustain the spiral of rising prices in the absence of increasing growth in the money supply. Thus, a sustained rise in the growth of money is a prerequisite for the existence of inflation.

Chart 5 / **Long-Run Cycles of Inflation and Money Growth per Decade (1750s–1970s)**

Except for the aftermath of the Civil War of the 1860s, the money-growth rate per decade reached its peak every third decade over more than two centuries, and so did the rate of inflation.

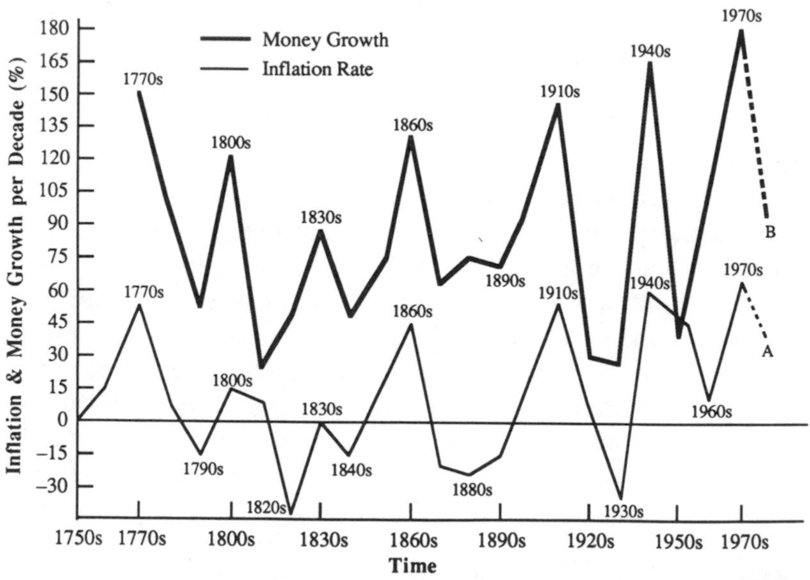

Source: See Appendix to Chapter 3.

Chart 5 confirms this result in a resounding way. It presents the paths of money growth and inflation together and shows that the two cycles run almost parallel. Not only do their peaks match, but they were also both disturbed in the aftermath of the Civil War. The chart thus clearly reveals that money growth is the primary determinant of the rate of inflation. Every decade during which money growth crests is also a decade when the rate of inflation crests.

5

THE LONG-RUN CYCLE OF REGULATION IN THE UNITED STATES

IT IS now commonly recognized that the main features of the economy during the 1970s were high inflation, high money growth, and high regulation of business by the government. With the onset of the 1980s, all three have declined. Why? Is this phenomenon merely a coincidence, or is it an integral part of certain trends in the U.S. economy?

We have already seen that money growth and inflation move together in terms of a decennial cycle cresting every third decade. What about the degree of economic regulation by the government? Does it also move in tandem with the cycles already examined? The answer, surprisingly, turns out to be yes.

Many today believe that the 1970s experienced an unprecedented growth in federal regulation. Between 1970 and 1980 twenty-one new regulatory agencies, with extensive powers to intervene in business decision-making of numerous industries, were established. The budget of the regulatory bodies expanded approximately 600 percent during this period, while their staffing level grew by over 300 percent. Thus, the 1970s indeed experienced tremendous growth in federal control over industry; yet this was not unprecedented. Tighter control had occurred during the 1940s, when the economy was caught in the throes of the Second World War. The much-touted regulatory growth during the New Deal era of the 1930s actually pales before that of the 1940s. Prior to that, in the decade between 1910 and 1920, the economy had also experienced a major surge in federal controls, caused not only by the First World War but also by the preceding turmoil in financial markets.

A close study of the U.S. economy reveals that the degree of regulation per decade has followed a cyclical path similar to that of money growth and inflation explored before. It, too, has crested every third decade except during the trauma following the Civil War.

Regulation may be defined as government interference in the decision-making process of the private sector. Examples of such interference are minimum wage laws, standards for product quality, statutes against discrimination in labor hiring, and so on. When a law is passed to regulate an industry, a federal agency is usually set up to oversee its enforcement. As of 1986 there were 138 federal regulatory bodies.

One way to measure the degree of regulation in the economy, then, is to determine the number of new regulatory agencies established per decade. The higher their number, the greater the degree of regulation during those years. Another way is to look at the number of major economic laws passed by Congress. As such laws proliferate, government intervention in the economy increases. In this broader measure, the regulation of business becomes synonymous with government interference with the operation of markets.

Increases in both these measures, of course, are compatible

with an economy expanding over time. If the economy grows but regulatory bodies do not, then the degree of regulation per unit of production will decline or deregulation will occur. The same is true with major economic laws. In a growing economy, therefore, the proper measure of regulation (or deregulation) is the number of new regulatory agencies created or of new economic laws passed per decade.[15] To be sure, one should also consider any agencies abolished or laws repealed. However, this seldom happens, and in what follows I examine only the new regulatory bodies established or the new economic measures passed per decade. This procedure, while simplifying the presentation, does not in any way invalidate my argument.

Consider Chart 6, which illustrates the time path of the two regulatory variables just described. (The data underlying

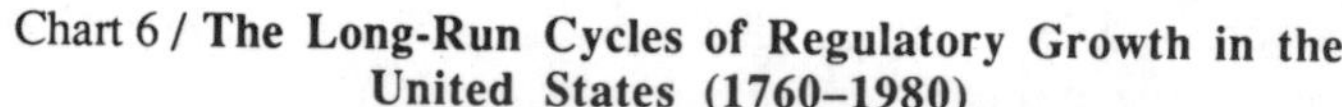

Chart 6 / **The Long-Run Cycles of Regulatory Growth in the United States (1760–1980)**

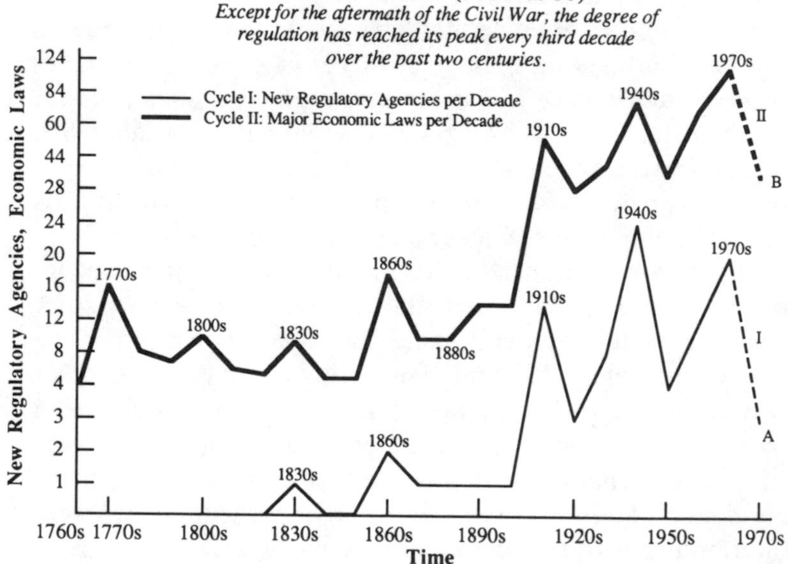

Source: See Appendix to Chapter 5.

them are presented in the Appendix to Chapter 5.) Both of them can be seen to be following a rhythmical pattern. Cycle I displays the path of the new regulatory agencies established per decade, beginning with the 1830s. The first federal regulatory body was established in 1836, so the 1830s constitute the first peak of this cycle. No agencies were created in the 1840s and 1850s but two were instituted in the 1860s, so that decade shows another peak in the decennial regulatory cycle.

Following the Civil War decade of the 1860s the cycle was disrupted, but resumed its normal path by cresting in the 1910s, 1940s, and 1970s. Point *A* in Chart 6 represents the new agencies created in the 1980s, assuming that the regulatory pace of the first four years of the Reagan Administration is maintained through the rest of the decade.

Thus, Cycle I shows that, except for the post–Civil War period, regulatory growth has followed an exact cycle, reaching a zenith every third decade.

Although the first regulatory body was not established until the 1830s, this does not mean that regulation was absent until that time. Congress had passed many economic laws even before, with significant impact on the course of the economy. Data for this broader measure of regulation date back to colonial times.

The time path of major economic laws per decade is illustrated in Chart 6 by Cycle II, beginning with the 1760s. Here the first peak occurs in the 1770s, following which economic legislation declines over the next two decades and crests again in the 1800s. Again it falls over the next two decades, rising to its zenith in the 1830s. This time the regulatory activity declines for only one decade, but still the subsequent peak occurs after thirty years in the 1860s, and so on. Again the 1910s, 1940s, and 1970s are the peak decades of Cycle II in the twentieth century, with point *B* representing the number of major economic laws projected for the 1980s.

It can be seen that the first index of regulation, the one

dealing with regulatory agencies, accords well with the fact that government control over the economy reached an all-time high during the 1940s, when wartime regulations were introduced in almost every sector. Prices, interest, wages, rents, and production were then controlled as never before or ever since. Although during the 1940s war was the main, if not the only, cause of regulation, during the 1910s regulation soared not only because of war, but also because of the preceding chaos in financial markets, which led to the creation of the Federal Reserve System in 1914. During the 1970s, by contrast, there was no major war but regulation peaked anyway. In other words, as with money growth and inflation, regulation tends to crest every third decade, but war is not its only cause.

Since the United States has been in the age of acquisitors ever since its birth, wealth has been the primary determinant of most variables in society, not just the economy. The fact that the cycle of regulation is totally dictated by the cycle of money growth proves this hypothesis empirically. In other words, *throughout U.S. history, money or wealth has been the nucleus around which revolve key social phenomena, including how the state governs its people.*

It may be noted that since regulation peaks every third decade, deregulation also occurs at the same intervals. This is because deregulation signifies a decline in regulatory growth or an outright fall in regulation.

Chart 6 does not reveal the full extent of deregulation that follows a war decade, because the economic laws passed to control the economy during the war are abolished in peacetime. There might actually be negative regulatory growth in some decades if the economic laws repealed fell short of the ones enacted during the ten-year period. Were this fact incorporated into the data, then each postwar decade, such as the 1780s, 1870s, 1920s, and 1950s, would turn out to be the peak decade of deregulation.

All this suggests that, except for the disruption caused by the Civil War, the degree of deregulation has also peaked every third decade ever since the birth of the nation. In view of this, it is not surprising that the 1980s are witnessing outright deregulation, not just an easing of regulation. Some regulatory bodies were actually abolished during the early 1980s, and budgets and staffing of others were reduced. Between 1980 and 1986, airlines, trucking, banking, railroads, telecommunications, and oil and natural gas were partially or wholly deregulated, while two federal agencies, the Cost Accounting Standards Board and the Civil Aeronautics Board, were terminated. Hence the 1980s are likely to be another peak decade of deregulation.

REGULATION, INFLATION, AND MONEY

A comparison of Chart 6 with Chart 5 in the previous chapter reveals that the long-run cycle of regulation has followed exactly the same pattern as the long-run decennial cycles of money growth and inflation. Every regulatory peak coincides with a peak decade of inflation and money growth. And when the inflation and money-growth cycles are disrupted, as in the post–Civil War period, the regulatory cycle is also disrupted. *This suggests that inflation is not only a monetary phenomenon, but is also a regulatory phenomenon.* In other words, high money growth is only one cause of inflation. The economic inefficiency generated by increased regulation also contributes to it.

Is there any connection between the cycles of money growth and regulation? It is very hard to uncover a symbiotic relationship between the two variables. The explanation according to the law of social cycles is, of course, that in the age of acquisitors, wealth or money growth is the major determinant of all social activity. Yet the relationship between money growth and regulation is not altogether obvious, for the two variables are controlled by different branches of government. The Federal Reserve System controls the supply of money, whereas regulatory agencies are created by Congress.

One possible explanation is that the forces which stimulate the growth of money also generate the need for increased regulation by government. For instance, many peaks of money growth occurred during wars. The 1770s, 1860s, 1910s, and 1940s were decades in which the nation was caught in major wars, which had to be financed through the printing of money. But these wars also generated the need for government control over the economy, for private consumption had to be restrained to pave the way for increased defense production. Hence high money growth and a major expansion of regulatory agencies coincided in war decades, because in both cases national survival was at stake.

Similarly, the 1970s experienced considerable expansion of both money supply and regulation. There was no major war in this decade, but the forces underlying the growth of the two variables were the same.

Ever since the Keynesian revolution, the pro-interventionist sentiment among intellectuals has been rising. This sentiment reached its peak in the 1970s mainly because of the socioeconomic problems created by an unprecedented rise in the price of oil. At the macro level, the interventionist argument is simply that the government is responsible for maintaining high employment, which has usually meant high money growth needed to finance expanding budget deficits. The same argument at the micro level is that the government is responsible for a clean environment, health and safety of workers, proper treatment of minorities by employers, antitrust and antimonopoly actions, and so on; and this spells further government regulation of business. Thus, in the 1970s there was no major war, but the interventionist bias was at its zenith. The result was a surge in both money growth and federal controls. History also reveals a high level of interventionist sentiment in the 1800s and 1830s, which were also peak decades of both money growth and regulation. This suggests that the reason why both money growth and regulation crest together is that they are stimulated by the same set of exogenous forces, such as war, interventionist demands, etc.

With Reagan's election in 1980 and 1984, the interventionist attitude has declined and the free-market sentiment is now on the rise. Hence both money growth and the degree of regulation have fallen below their levels during the 1970s.

Current economic theory ignores the influence of regulation on inflation and focuses mainly on the annual rate of money growth. Monetarism has won over the experts, at least as far as the question of inflation is concerned. Anytime the Federal Reserve announces that the money supply is growing above its recent average, forecasts come pouring out, warning of the resurgence of inflation. This obsession with money has led to faulty predictions from prominent economists, including Milton Friedman. In an article in *The Wall Street Journal* in 1984, Lindley Clark and Laurie McGinley wrote: "Late last year, Milton Friedman predicted a recession in the first half of 1984 and soaring inflation in the second half. He was dead wrong: The economy boomed in the first half, and there aren't any indications of a major recession in the second."[16]

The reason why inflation has fallen much more than the decline in money growth in the 1980s is that major deregulation is now under way. Deregulation promotes a competitive environment in which businessmen find it difficult to raise prices at will. Nor can labor unions win inflationary wage increases. Moreover, the long-run decennial cycle of inflation is now in its downswing, but the experts have failed to recognize this trend. That is why I think that even their long-run forecasts will be wrong. Economist Ralph Winter reports that "the consensus forecast of a group of 47 leading economists . . . is for a 5.3% annual rise in the consumer price index for 1985–89 and a slightly lower 5.1% yearly rise from 1990 through 1994."[17]

This forecast is inconsistent with the long-run cycle of inflation. In my view, the annual rate of inflation during the 1980s will hover around 3.5 percent, but the 1990s might even experience deflation, which means negative inflation. Between 1990 and 1994, prices could actually fall, as we shall see in the next chapter and Chapter 8.

6

CONCENTRATION OF WEALTH AND DEPRESSIONS

UNTIL 1929, the fateful year of the "Great Crash," a name coined by John Kenneth Galbraith, few economists were interested in the question of unemployment. They had been reared in the classical tradition and regarded business downturns and the attendant loss of jobs as temporary phenomena, to be replaced by prosperity and boom within one or two years.

Since then economics has undergone major surgery, and volume upon volume have appeared, attributing depressions to a bewildering variety of casual factors. However, as I shall presently explain, even now few economists truly understand what causes a depression. In this respect, the situation is hardly different from that in the 1920s. As before, economic theory is ill-prepared to deal with impending catastrophe.

My argument is that depressions, as distinct from recessions, are caused by an extreme concentration of wealth.

However, the subject of wealth disparity is more or less a taboo among established economists and those in power. Just look into the top ten economic journals over the past fifty years and you will find less than one percent of space devoted to this question. This is really unfortunate, because faulty economic thought frequently leads to economic disasters.

The ebb and flow that periodically occurs in the GNP is commonly called the business cycle, which has characterized Western economies for as far back as records exist. Economic activity usually passes through four phases—recession, depression, recovery, and boom. When the GNP and employment are declining, the economy is said to be in a recession, which, when deep, becomes a depression. When output and employment are rising, the economy is said to be in a phase of recovery, which becomes a boom as full employment nears and industries operate at maximum capacity.

A recession usually lasts for one to three years during which the rate of unemployment, while rising, is generally below 12 percent. When a recession lasts for more than three years, and/or the rate of unemployment lies between 12 percent and 20 percent, the economy may be said to be suffering from a depression. When unemployment remains high and business stagnates for six or more years, the nation's plight may be called a great depression. Thus, depending on its severity in depth and length, the downswing of the business cycle may be defined as a recession, depression, or a great depression.

All business contractions are bad, but depressions are disastrous and great depressions simply cataclysmic. As prosperous as the U.S. economy has been since the Second World War, it too has passed through all types of convulsions in its long history. It has frequently faced recessions, at times depressions, and, rarely, great depressions. This is a plague that has haunted Western society for a long time, and economists have periodically offered various cures. Yet the theory of business contraction is still seriously deficient, and despite the appearance of hundreds of hypotheses, all that economists have really done is to provide a theory of recession, not of depression. However, before analyzing this issue, let us explore the historical record.

THE PATTERN OF DEPRESSIONS

We have seen that, except in the aftermath of the Civil War, inflation, regulation, and money growth in the U.S. economy have crested together every third decade over more than two centuries. These may be called regular or deterministic cycles because they adhere to the concept of historical determinism. Is there an identical cycle with respect to business activity or the GNP? The answer is no. Yet a similar pattern can be detected in the history of the U.S. economy.

In the U.S. economy there has been at least one recession every decade, and a great depression every third or sixth decade in the sense that if the third decade managed to avoid a depression, then the sixth decade experienced a cumulative effect—an all-out disaster. Thus the 1780s witnessed a depression, but the 1810s did not. Three decades later, the 1840s passed through an unprecedented crisis. The 1870s also suffered a great depression, but the 1900s did not. Then thirty years later there occurred the greatest depression in history.

The Depression of the 1780s

Data about American business activity, as reported by the Cleveland Trust Company (now Ameri Trust Company), go as far back as 1790. For the 1780s, we have to rely on contemporary writings and books on history.

The course of the American economy in the 1770s was determined mainly by the Revolution. Although there was a lot of destruction in some regions, many farmers and merchants prospered greatly from the war. Those who were dependent on British markets were the big losers, as these markets were closed to their products. However, those who could sell their goods to British or American troops profited handsomely from the hostilities. On the whole, the American economy flourished because of the war.

After the British defeat at Yorktown in October 1781, a downturn set in. Business activity began to decline in 1782, and after the peace treaty was signed in Paris in 1783, the economy slid into a depression, which was caused mainly by a huge deficit in the balance of trade. There was a great influx of British goods, which were in heavy demand in the free nation. But they also depressed prices in American markets. Foreign markets, because of protectionist policies of Britain and France, were not fully open to American goods. As a result, exports fell far short of imports, causing a massive deficit in the U.S. balance of trade and a serious depression.

Although the economy began to move out of its slump in 1786, farm prices remained depressed well into 1787. Thus, from start to finish, the depression of the 1780s lasted five to six years, from 1782–83 to 1787—qualifying it as a serious, though perhaps not a great, depression.

The Great Depression of the 1840s

The record of business cycles from 1790 to 1980 is illustrated in Charts 7 to 9, which deal with fluctuations in business activity around a long-term trend. If every year the economy grew at a constant rate, then its expansion path when graphed would be a straight line, which is called a trend line or the line of zero deviation. The vertical axis in the charts measures percentage oscillations, positive or negative,

Chart 7 / **Business Cycles 1790–1855**

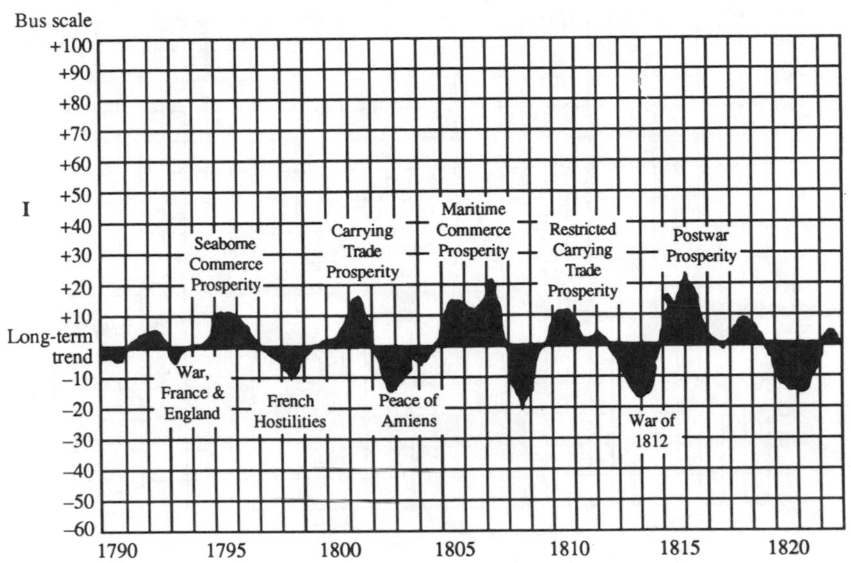

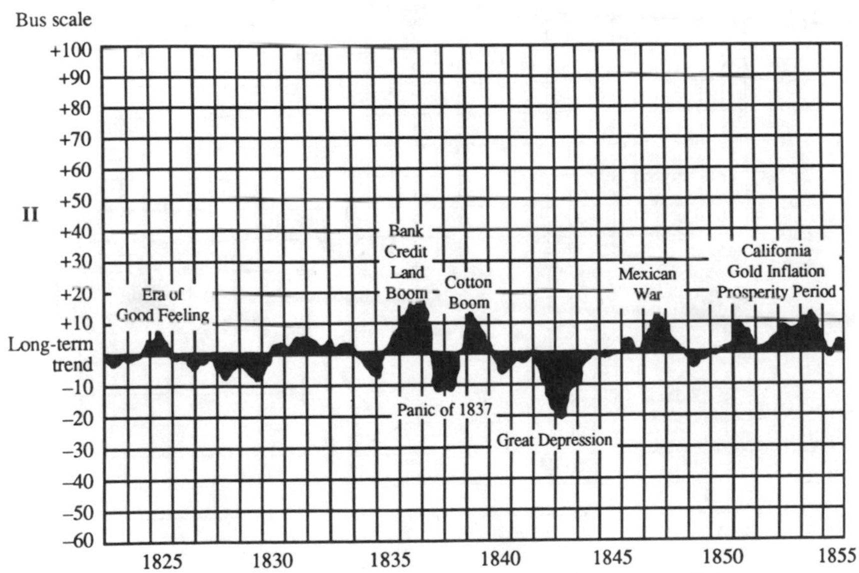

Source: Adapted from Ameri Trust Company's Annual Report.

Chart 8 / **Business Cycles 1855–1920**

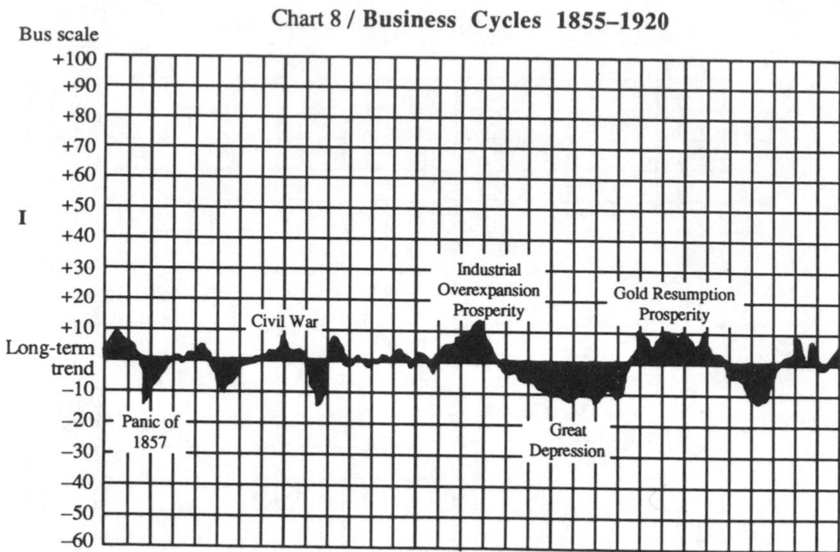

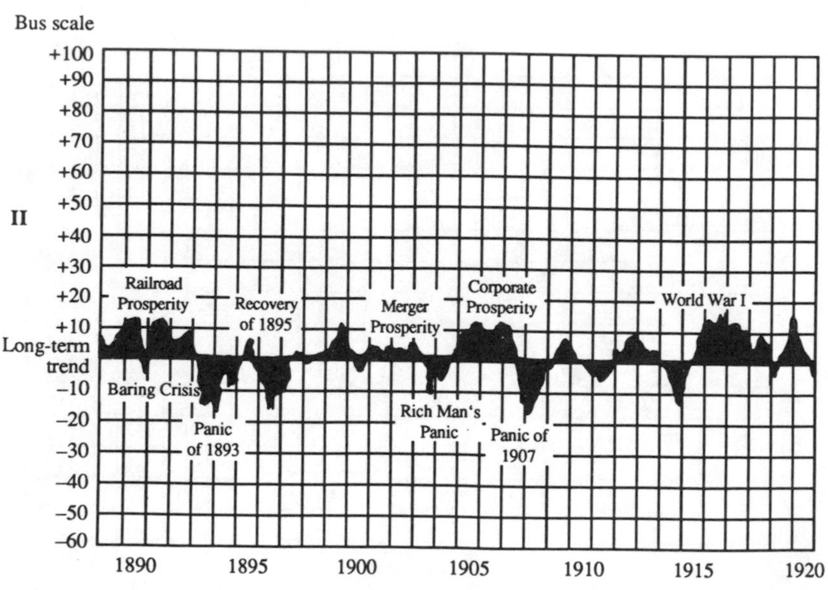

Source: Adapted from Ameri Trust Company's Annual Report.

Chart 9 / **Business Cycles 1920–1980**

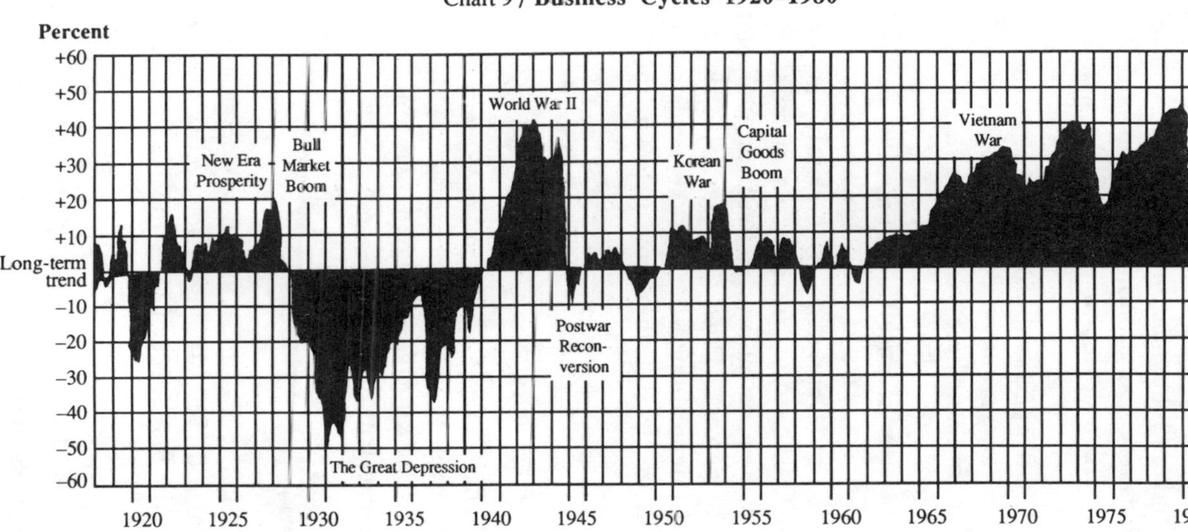

Source: Adapted from the Ameri Trust Company's Annual Report.

from the trend, and the horizontal axis represents time. Positive deviations reflect an economy in the upward phase of the cycle, and negative deviations represent economic contractions.

Part I of Chart 7 shows that between 1790 and 1820 there were many recessions but no depression, because no downturn lasted more than three years. Part II, however, reveals that the slump of the 1840s endured for seven years, from 1840 through 1846, because throughout this period business activity was below the trend line. This contraction, called the Debt Repudiation Depression, was clearly the worst until that time in U.S. history. Not only was it painfully long, it was also very deep, as business activity, at one point, fell by more than 20 percent. Thus, the disaster of the 1840s was clearly a great depression. Note that there was no depression in the 1810s, or at any other time between the 1790s and 1830s.

The Great Depression of the 1870s

Part I of Chart 8 reveals a seven-year slump in the 1870s, three decades after the previous depression. This contraction began in 1873 and afflicted the economy through 1879. This, too, was a great depression.

The Great Depression of the 1930s

Part II of Chart 8 reveals that there was no great depression between 1890 and 1920, although two severe slumps occurred in the 1890s, the first between 1893 and 1895 and the other in 1896–97.

Let us now consider Chart 9, which plots business cycles between 1920 and 1980, and shows that the 1930s experienced the worst depression of all time. This calamity was the longest—economic activity remained below the trend line for ten years—as well as the deepest in history, because the economy at one point sank more than 40 percent below the trend line.

Here again, it may be noted that the 1910s experienced no depression of any kind. Nor has there been a depression since 1940. There were minor recessions between 1945 and 1960, and between 1960 and 1980 there were severe slumps but no depression, as the annual rate of unemployment never exceeded 9 percent. The highest rate of unemployment since the Second World War was recorded at the end of 1982, when it approached 11 percent. In other words, there has been no depression in America since the 1930s, although serious recessions did occur in the 1970s and between 1980 and 1982.

Thus the record shows that there have been three great depressions in the United States, in the 1840s, 1870s, and 1930s, and the slump of the 1780s, though perhaps not a great depression, was unprecedented as it lingered for five or six years. Of these four, two were the deepest in history. The depressions of the 1840s and the 1930s were the worst in memory. So, even though—unlike inflation, money growth, and regulation, which have jointly crested every third decade—depressions do not have an exact cycle, they have indeed followed a pattern which in a way accords with the three-decade cycle, as seen below.

The 1780s experienced a depression, but the 1810s (three decades later) did not, nor did any other decade until the 1840s (six decades later), which witnessed a great depression that was the deepest until that time. Thirty years later, the 1870s also passed through a great depression, but this was not as severe as the calamity of the 1840s. Another great depression was due in the 1900s, but none appeared at that time. Hence three decades later occurred the greatest depression in history.

Conventional Wisdom on Depressions

What causes recessions and depressions? This question has haunted Western society for more than two centuries, eliciting a wide variety of theories and conjectures from economists. Yet all that the experts have really produced so far is a general theory of a recession rather than a depression.

The conventional wisdom essentially rests on the Keynesian mechanism determining a country's GNP, something we first analyzed in Chapter 3. Although the concepts of aggregate demand and aggregate supply introduced by Keynes have been greatly modified over the years, his basic premise remains intact. There is now general agreement that the business cycle in American history has been propelled mainly by fluctuations in aggregate demand for goods and services rather than by fluctuations in aggregate supply. Some downturns may indeed have been initiated by supply-side disturbances, such as the sharp increase in oil prices in the 1970s, yet, by and large, recessions and depressions have been caused by a contraction in aggregate demand.

Up to this point both Keynesians and Monetarists agree. Where they part company is on the question of the main source of fluctuations in aggregate demand, which consists of total consumption, investment, and government expenditure. Monetarists believe that money is the primary determinant of aggregate spending. When the Fed adds to the ability of the banking system to increase the supply of money, the private sector is able to borrow more funds than before at an acceptable rate of interest, and this in turn induces a rise in aggregate demand. This line of reasoning, then, establishes a strong connection between money supply and business activity. Monetarists believe that major recessions have been associated with absolute declines in money supply and minor ones with contractions in money growth.

In support of their view, Monetarists cite the experience of the economy during the Great Depression of the 1930s. The stock market crash in October 1929 generated a great deal of uncertainty in the public, which reacted by increasing its withdrawal of cash from the banks. The Fed, which had been set up mainly to enable the system to meet such exigencies, failed to rescue the banks, which were basically sound but were unable to meet the public's sudden demand for cash. As a result, many banks failed, and in turn brought ruin to their depositors, who were forced to curtail their spending. This, of course, led to successive declines in business activity. Nearly two thousand banks suspended operations in 1931 alone. The collapse of the banking system, while the Fed stood idly by, caused a sharp drop in the money supply, which between 1929 and 1932 fell by more than a third.

Keynesians accept this scenario of the monetary collapse sketched by Monetarists. They agree that the Fed behavior in the 1930s was misguided. But they argue that instead of the falling money supply ushering in the decline in the GNP, the falling GNP could have caused the decline in money supply. This is a chicken-and-egg question: Which came first? Keynesians challenge the causality that Monetarists impute to money and the GNP during the Great Depression. In support of their view, they cite the experience of the Canadian and British economies in the 1930s. The central banks in both Britain and Canada came to the rescue of their banking systems, and as a result bank failures were minor. Yet their economies, especially Canada's, were traumatized just as much as the U.S. economy. Therefore the drop in the money supply could not have been so crucial to the severity of the Great Depression.

To Keynesians, the Great Depression was initiated in 1929 by a drop in investment and made worse by the inept fiscal policy of the government. As business activity fell, tax revenues declined. In order to balance its budget, the government raised tax rates, and this, according to Keynesians, was a defective policy, as higher taxes forced the public to further reduce its consumption, leading to a further fall in the GNP, and so on. Therefore, the recession of 1929 developed into a depression because of the dubious fiscal policy of the government.

A synthetic view is that both monetary and fiscal policies were inept during the 1930s, and that they turned what otherwise could have been a mild recession into the greatest depression ever. Thus conventional wisdom blames the catastrophe of the 1930s on mistaken policies of the government. There are, however, a few facts that economists have slighted or ignored.

Concentration of Wealth and Depressions

True, monetary and fiscal policies were faulty at the time of the Great Depression. But were they not faulty at the time of every major recession of the nineteenth century? Friedman, the patriarch of the Monetarists, himself argues that money growth decreased during every recession in the nineteenth century. Similarly, Keynesians recognize that in every recession before the Second World War, the government tended to balance its budget by raising taxes. The accepted doctrine in the pre-Keynesian days, after all, was that, as with a prudent household, the government's expenses ought not to exceed its income. Therefore if tax revenue falls, as it usually does during a downturn, the government should either trim its expenditures, raise taxes, or both. Hence fiscal policy tended in the past to be restrictive whenever a recession occurred.

Clearly, then, both monetary and fiscal policies failed to

deal adequately with the recessions of the past. There was nothing new about the remedies that were applied to the recession of 1929. Why, then, did it turn into the greatest economic calamity ever? In plain words, the issue is simply this: If faulty government policies did not create a major depression in the past, why did they create one in the 1930s? There must have been some new factor at work in 1929. There must have been some other parameter which has eluded the experts so far.

There is a large body of economic literature upholding the theory that recessions are caused by unequal distribution of income. Keynes himself pointed this out as one reason for the rise in savings and hence a decline in aggregate demand. As savings rise, consumption falls by the same amount. Since the rich have a higher propensity to save than the poor, concentration of income in a few hands induces an increase in aggregate savings.

Now, savings did increase as income inequality rose during the 1920s. Much of the population had failed to share in the national prosperity. However, most economists agree that this rise in savings was not sharp enough to generate a crisis of the magnitude of the Great Crash. It was perhaps sufficient to initiate a recession, but not a cataclysm severe enough to engulf the whole world.

The wave of business mergers that occurred during the 1920s is sometimes cited as another cause of the Great Depression. Many monopolies, oligopolies, and other industrial giants had emerged almost overnight to induce a highly inefficient economy. This led to a fall in investment and hence in aggregate demand. But here again the fall was not large enough to generate a worldwide crisis of these proportions. Indeed, such industrial concentration had occurred before, especially during the 1880s and late 1890s, but had not produced an economic disaster.

What, then, was the real cause of the Great Depression? What is the parameter that has so far escaped the economic theorists?

My contention is that this parameter was the concentration of wealth, not just of income, which peaked in 1929 and gave rise to the Great Depression. While the concentration of income indeed had played a role, it alone could not have caused the grave crisis, for the aggregate level of wealth far exceeds national income at any point of time.

During the 1920s there was a sudden sharp surge in the inequality of the distribution of wealth. Table 1 shows that in 1922 1 percent of U.S. families owned 31.6 percent of national wealth, but by 1929, only seven years later, their share

TABLE 1

Share of Wealth Held by the Richest 1 Percent

Year	Share of Wealth Held by 1 Percent of U.S. Adults or Families
1810	21.0
1860	24.0
1870	27.0
1900	26.0–31.0
1922	31.6
1929	36.3
1933	28.3
1939	30.6
1945	23.3
1949	20.8
1953	27.5
1956	26.0
1958	26.9
1962	27.4
1963	31.6
1965	29.2
1969	24.9
1983	34.3

Source: See note 19.

had risen to 36.3 percent. This represents a gigantic leap in the concentration of wealth, which, barring some unprecedented disturbance or misguided fiscal policy, usually moves at a slow, almost glacial rate, with shifts measured in a very small percentage over a long period of time. For instance, between 1933 and 1969 the share of top wealth-holders varied between 28.3 percent and 24.9 percent—a fairly small variation. Their share, of course, dropped drastically between 1929 and 1933, as a direct result of the Great Depression wiping out many fortunes. In addition to the sharp rise in inequality of wealth in just seven years during the 1920s, the share of the top wealth-holders in 1929 was the highest in history.

What is the connection between the unequal distribution of wealth and a depression? To understand this, it is necessary to reexamine the difference between a recession and a depression. A recession occurs when, because of a drop in demand, the GNP begins to fall or its growth fails to keep pace with the growth in the labor force, so that the rate of unemployment begins to rise. A depression occurs when a recession is accompanied by a collapse of the financial system, so that demand continues to drop precipitously over several years. Many businesses then vanish, the public loses confidence in banks, and unemployment climbs to levels unprecedented in recent memory. In other words, a one-time drop in demand is not enough to cause a depression.

By failing to explain why demand continues to decline, current economic thought deals only with a recession but not a depression. As Galbraith puts it so eloquently in the context of the Great Depression: "First there is the question of why economic activity turned down in 1929. Second there is the vastly more important question of why, having started down, on this unhappy occasion it went down and down and down and remained low for a full decade."[18] Traditional economics answers the first question but not the "vastly more important" second question.

U.S. history reveals that in a recession, unemployment climbs no higher than 12 percent, whereas in a depression it may go as high as 25 percent. As noted before, there have been numerous recessions in the United States but only three great depressions, and each time it was the massive run on the banks that turned an ordinary fall in the GNP into a disaster.

What causes a financial panic? To understand this, let us examine the behavior of a typical bank, which, we assume, is interested in making loans at the highest possible interest rate so that its profits are maximized. Normally the bank lends money to credit-worthy individuals or businesses, which are unlikely to default on the loan. But at times, the bank may make risky loans with a high potential for failure. This happens especially when competition among banks is high in securing borrowers or deposits.

When wealth becomes concentrated, three effects normally occur. First, the number of persons with few or no assets rises. As a result the demand for loans increases, because the borrowing needs of the poor and middle-income groups far exceed those of the affluent. Second, since the poor and the middle class, who are in a majority, now have fewer assets, the borrowers in general become less credit-worthy than before. If a bank rejects risky borrowers, its financial structure remains sound. But in an environment where creditworthiness has generally deteriorated, most banks cannot afford to be choosy, especially when they have to pay interest on their deposits. Only a prudent bank then avoids making risky loans. Thus, as the concentration of wealth rises, the number of banks with relatively shaky loans also rises. And the higher the concentration, the greater the number of potential bank failures.

A side effect of the growing wealth disparity is the rise in speculative investments. As a person becomes wealthy, his aversion to risk declines.[20] As wealth inequality grows, the overall riskiness of investments made by the rich also grows.

It essentially reflects the human urge to make a quick profit. It means margin or installment buying of assets and goods only for resale and not for productive purposes. It means, for instance, increasing involvement of investors in futures markets. When others see the rich profiting quickly from speculative purchases, they tend to follow suit. As Charles Kindleberger aptly puts it:

> When the number of firms and households indulging in these practices grows large, bringing in segments of population that are normally aloof from such ventures, speculation for profit leads away from such normal, rational behavior to what have been described as "manias" or "bubbles." The word "mania" emphasizes the irrationality; "bubble" foreshadows the bursting.
>
> . . . The object of speculation may vary widely from one mania or bubble to the next. It may involve primary products, or goods manufactured for export to distant markets, domestic and foreign securities of various kinds, contracts to buy or sell goods or securities, land in the country or city, houses, office buildings, shopping centers, condominiums, foreign exchange. At a late stage, speculation tends to detach itself from really valuable objects and turn to delusive ones. A larger and larger group of people seeks to become rich without a real understanding of the process involved. Not surprisingly swindlers and catchpenny schemes flourish.[21]

As Kindleberger points out, speculative fever tends to feed on itself, and by the time the general population rushes to join the bandwagon, the venture is usually nearing its last stage.

Unless one has money to spare, one cannot participate in speculative markets. Risky investments often pay off in a healthy economy, and gradually people in increasing numbers are lured into the game. Eventually even those normally too cautious for such ventures are tempted by "easy" profits. However, the speculative fever cannot begin in the absence of wealth disparity, for only the very rich can afford to squander money on investments with a high but relatively illusive return. They alone can initiate the fever. In other words, wealth inequality is a prerequisite for manias and bubbles. The greater the inequity, the bigger the bubble and the more painful its eventual bursting.

In short, the concentration of wealth has two pernicious effects on the economy: it increases the number of banks with shaky loans, and fuels the speculative frenzy in which eventually even the banking system is caught.

As long as the economy is healthy, borrowers are in a position to pay back the loans and the financial system goes on functioning smoothly. However, as soon as aggregate demand falls for any reason, some goods go unsold, business inventories rise, output falls, and some workers are laid off. A few businesses and banks begin to fail. This, of course, typically occurs during a recession. Inventories are soon depleted as output declines faster than demand. As the economy improves, producers gradually regain confidence to raise production and recall fired workers, with the economy resuming its path of expansion.

The depth of a recession depends on the extent of prevailing wealth disparity that raises the number of fragile banks and feeds speculation. Whenever a bank fails, there occurs some decrease in total deposits and money supply and hence a further decrease in aggregate demand and output. Therefore, higher concentration of wealth, by increasing the number of fragile banks, produces a deeper recession.

Under capitalism wealth disparity tends to rise in the long run. A time comes when this disparity, and the concomitant number of shaky banks, becomes so great that any recession can cause a collapse of the financial system. The bursting of the speculative bubble, another direct consequence of the inequity, only adds fuel to the fire. Money supply, aggregate demand, output, and employment then move in a downward spiral, and an ordinary recession turns into a depression. If the speculative bubble is extremely large, then its bursting gives rise to a great depression. In the aftermath, the concentration of wealth declines, because many fortunes have been wiped out.

Great inequality in wealth does not develop overnight. It derives mainly from inheritance. Usually it takes at least a generation before wealth is transferred to posterity and its distribution becomes critically unequal. That is why we find that while there have been many recessions in American history, depressions have been rare, usually separated by one or two generations.

Table 1 shows that the wealth disparity in 1929 was the steepest ever. Speculative loans made by the banks were also at their zenith at that time. It is no wonder, then, that an ordinary recession in 1929 turned into an unprecedented economic disaster.

Since the 1930s, wealth disparity has been generally on the decline, although it began to rise again in the 1980s. That is why the economy has succeeded in avoiding depressions, though it has had a close brush with severe recessions, such as the periods 1973–75 and 1980–82.

Table 1 shows that the disparity of wealth was also high in 1870, when, as the record reveals, there occurred a wave of speculation in railroad securities and in the New York stock market, which eventually crashed in September 1873, leading to the great depression of the 1870s.

For the 1840s we lack any precise figure on the disparity of wealth. However, Jeffrey Williamson and Peter Lindert conclude that "the wealth concentration rose over most of the period 1774–1860, with especially steep increases from the 1830s to the late 1840s."[22] What evidence there is points to the fact that there was a sharp jump in wealth inequality during the

1830s, which experienced a speculative frenzy in land and cotton, culminating in the crisis of 1839 and the great depression of the 1840s.

Thus, while conventional wisdom may provide a theory of recession—that it is caused by a decline in aggregate demand—it lacks an adequate explanation for the surge of speculative manias that has always preceded an economic crisis. It also fails to explain the fragility of the banking system, which collapses to generate a financial panic. Both these effects spring from high wealth disparity. Hence the real cause of great depressions in the past, or of depressions of any kind, was not faulty government policies but extreme inequality in the distribution of wealth. A depression, in a nutshell, is the result of a financial panic accompanying a recession.

Perverse Fiscal Policy of the 1920s

Keynesians contend that the fiscal policy of the early 1930s was faulty, as the government attempted to balance its budget by raising taxes, whereas it should have done just the opposite to stimulate aggregate demand. There is no doubt that this type of fiscal action worsened the situation, but without a fragile financial system it could not have caused the catastrophe. A crisis such as a depression does not occur overnight. It requires several years of fiscal mismanagement.

The seeds of the Great Depression were actually sown by the truly faulty fiscal policies of the 1920s, when the government reduced taxes in 1921, 1924, 1926, and 1928. These tax cuts were very favorable to big business and high-income groups. The concentration of wealth was already high in the early 1920s, when, as Table 1 reveals, barely one percent of U.S. families owned almost a third of national wealth. Reducing the taxes of the rich was, then, a clearly misguided policy. There is nothing wrong with cutting taxes and reducing the size of the government. Big government adds to economic inefficiency and mismanagement. But easing the tax burden of the multimillionaires—that is something else. Nothing but increasing wealth disparity and hence eventual calamity can come from it.

The result was inevitable. The tax cuts of the 1920s generated the sharpest rise ever in wealth concentration in just a matter of seven years. Between 1922 and 1929, the rich became richer as never before. As a consequence, the banking system was the shakiest and the speculative bubble the largest in history. So was the eventual collapse of the economy.

Thus, while the fiscal policy of the early 1930s was mistaken, the truly disastrous tax policy had already occurred in the 1920s, when the reduced tax burden of the affluent planted the seeds of the Great Crash.

7

THE GREAT DEPRESSION OF 1990–96

IT IS time to weave the various strands together and see what we have learned from history, which, as is clear by now, has its own rhythm. We have discovered that inflation, money growth, and regulation have all followed a clear-cut and deterministic path, and though the behavior of great depressions is not so apparent, they too have had a definite pattern. While the cycles of inflation, money growth, and regulation have all crested together every third decade for over two centuries, great depressions have occurred at intervals of three or six decades.

The burning question that now concerns the lives and future of each of us is: Can it happen again? Is another great depression possible? This thought, which comes up every time the economy is in distress, has haunted the public since the early 1970s, when a sharp surge in the price of oil generated the most serious recession since the Second World

War. It is an issue that has revived interest in the theory of the business cycle, which many in the 1960s regarded as obsolete; however, the cycle is well and alive. It has recently inspired a spate of books by some notable thinkers.[23]

Much of the new energy is directed at understanding what really caused the depression of the 1930s. Few directly address themselves to the question: Is another great depression possible? My answer is that not only is another 1930s-style tragedy possible, it is, given the perverse fiscal policy of the Reagan presidency, inevitable. But before I explain why, let us review the conventional wisdom regarding this question.

Rudiger Dornbusch and Stanley Fischer, authors of one of the best-selling texts on macroeconomics, speak of the unlikely recurrence of a great depression:

> On the question of whether it could happen again, there is agreement that it could not, except, of course, in the event of truly perverse policies. But these are less likely now than they were then. For one thing we have history to help us avoid its repetition. Taxes would not again be raised in the middle of a depression nor would attempts be made to balance the budget. The Fed would seek actively to keep the money supply from falling. In addition, the government now has a much larger role in the economy than it did then. The high level of government spending, which is relatively slow to change, and automatic stabilizers, including the income tax, unemployment insurance, and Social Security, give the economy more stability than it had then.[24]

In a front-page article entitled "Economists Don't See Threats to Economy Portending Depression," *The Wall Street Journal* echoed the same sentiment. There Lindley Clark and Alfred Malabre, reflecting the majority view of economists, concluded that "the public should have—if anything—more confidence than before that an economic crackup like that in the 1930s won't happen again. That at least is the judgment of 10 eminent analysts."[25] The article reflects the opinion of, among others, three Nobel laureates and two former chiefs of the Federal Reserve Board. According to the *Journal,* this group has consistently maintained that another 1930s-style calamity is not likely. Paul Samuelson, a Nobel laureate, is quoted as saying, "Another depression on the order of the 1930s just doesn't seem possible." The attitude of Arthur Burns, the Fed chairman under Presidents Nixon, Ford, and Carter, is much the same. The *Journal* reports him as saying, "I still see no new Great Depression in the cards for the simple reason that the government can prevent collapse, and the government will prevent it." In addition to these eminent authorities, the *Journal* cites Geoffrey Moore, William Martin, Milton Friedman, Lawrence Klein, Martin Feldstein, Robert Hall, and Charles Kindleberger as equally convinced that another great depression is not in prospect.

These economists are among the best that the profession has to offer. They certainly have made great contributions to our understanding of economics. Some of them are also concerned about government actions. Martin fears the detrimental effects of financial deregulation, while Friedman is apprehensive about the consequences of international debt, and Feldstein is concerned about unprecedented budget deficits. Many of them are anxious about growing demands for protectionist trade barriers.

They are all, however, quite optimistic about the future course of the American economy. While they may disagree over the true cause of the Great Depression, they are all convinced that such an event is unlikely to recur—at least not in the near future. Usual reasons cited for their optimism are that the government will not repeat the policy mistakes of the 1930s. Taxes will not again be raised in the midst of a recession, nor will the money supply be allowed to fall so sharply.

Since 1984, however, the year the *Wall Street Journal* article voiced the opinion of the ten notable economists, there has been a good deal of debate over the possibility of another crash.[26] Some of those who had long been optimistic about future prosperity now concede a slim chance to the occurrence of another calamity. It may be that the experts interviewed by the *Journal* have now changed their views. They certainly have identified troubled areas in the economy, but are perhaps reluctant to take the final step and recognize the severity of the impending disaster. In any case, I am convinced, more now than ever before, that if nothing is done at this time, then history is soon going to repeat itself.

The testimony of the long-run cycles presented in earlier chapters points to only one direction, namely that another economic disaster, possibly worse than the 1930s catastrophe, is now in the making. The cycles of money, inflation, and regulation and the pattern of great depressions are remarkable for their longevity and antiquity. They have survived phenomenal changes in the American economy and society. They have persisted through industrial revolutions, breathtaking new technology, two world wars, waves of regulation and business mergers, the creation of the Fed, the New Deal, the atomic age, the gold standard, the dollar standard, and myriad social movements. And that which has persisted so long amid numerous convulsions is likely to persist in the future as well. Barring another Civil War, the stranglehold of these cycles can be broken only by fundamental economic reforms.

RELATIONSHIP AMONG CYCLES

Let us see what the essential message of the long-run cycles is as it relates to the law of social cycles. I have argued that ever since the 1860s the West has been in its second age of acquisitors. This age reached its zenith in the 1920s. That is why the Great Depression only produced economic calamity but not political change, as the affluent have continued to dominate society. But since the 1930s the influence of acquisitors has been on the decline in the sense that not the rich themselves but their hired intellectuals have been running the machinery of government. Hence if a depression occurs in the near future, not only will the economy collapse, but the political structure will also be transformed.

Every age passes through two phases—the rising phase and the declining phase. During the ascending period, the dominant class is clearly on top and its reign is more or less unchallenged. During the descending period, troubles begin to mount and the leaders turn to intellectuals for advice. Hence during the declining phase the dominant class continues to rule but only with the help of advisers belonging to the class of intellectuals. And during the downswing of the acquisitive era, the intellectuals also turn into acquisitors.

Since the 1930s there has been a rise in pro-interventionist sentiment, which maintains that it is the government's responsibility to cure social ills. But in order to translate this idea into reality, intellectuals are needed first to devise and then to enforce regulations. That is why it is the intellectual acquisitor, rather than the "pure" acquisitor, who has been dominant in Western society since the 1930s. This is the surest sign that the age of acquisitors has been in the downswing ever since, and may be ready to breathe its last.

With the age of acquisitors on the downturn, a major economic crisis today would trigger a political upheaval in the West. During the 1920s the era of the wealthy was at its zenith; therefore all that the Great Crash did was to transfer power from "pure" acquisitors to intellectual acquisitors. But there was no change in the dominant class itself, as supermaterialism, the basic ideology of acquisitors, continued to permeate the social psyche. However, if a catastrophe hits the economy in the future, a new class will come to power.

In Chapters 3 and 4, we showed that the U.S. economy, except in the aftermath of the Civil War, has over the past two centuries experienced long-run cycles of inflation and money growth, jointly peaking every third decade. Since such a peak last appeared in the 1970s, we can expect that, barring another cataclysm on the order of the Civil War, the 1990s will experience sharply lower money growth and further disinflation, if not outright deflation.

In Chapter 5, we demonstrated that the U.S. economy has also experienced a long-run decennial cycle of regulation which jointly crests with the other two cycles. Moreover, at least during the twentieth century, the peak years of regulation have been followed by a decade of deregulation, and then by another surge in regulation reflected in socioeconomic reforms, culminating in high inflation. Thus the regulatory cycle crested in the 1910s, bottomed in the 1920s, only to start rising again in the 1930s. It crested again in the 1940s, bottomed in the 1950s, and resumed its climb in the 1960s. In the 1970s, it peaked again. The 1980s, not surprisingly, are experiencing deregulation; similarly, the 1990s will be a decade of socioeconomic reforms leading to another rise in regulation.

During the 1930s, economic institutions were reformed under the New Deal; during the 1960s, social and economic institutions underwent reforms stimulated by the civil rights movement. Since the regulatory cycle, under the influence of intellectual acquisitors, reveals an upward trend, reforms of the 1990s will not only be social and economic, but political as well, leading to a possible overhaul of the Constitution. This means that society will then be traumatized in more spheres than occurred in the 1930s and 1960s. Why else would it need reforms in so many areas? The cycle of regulation, therefore, corresponds with the law of social cycles.

In Chapter 6, I have argued that wealth disparity gives rise to a shaky banking system and to a speculative bubble that bursts when a recession hits. The combination of a recession and the collapse of the banking system generates a depression. In 1929, the disparity in wealth was at its zenith, with just 1 percent of U.S. families owning over 36 percent of national wealth. Consequently, the 1930s experienced an all-time economic disaster, accompanied by the sharpest deflation ever.

In this chapter, I also demonstrated that, as with money, inflation, and regulation, great depressions too have followed the third-decade/sixth-decade pattern. The 1780s witnessed a serious depression, but the 1810s did not. Hence the 1840s underwent the worst depression of the times. The 1870s also suffered a great depression, but the 1900s did not. Hence the 1930s went through a carnage worse than ever before.

The Depression of the 1990s

The message of cycles must now be crystal clear. Since the 1960s escaped a great depression, the 1990s will experience another cumulative effect—the worst economic crisis in history.

The seeds of this calamity have already been planted by the misguided fiscal policy of the Reagan Administration. During the 1920s, the pro-business, pro-affluent tax cuts caused a sharply higher concentration of wealth, which eventually led to the collapse of the economy. During the 1980s, the tax cuts of 1981 and 1986 are producing the same effects. The disparity in wealth is now climbing at an unprecedented pace.

Within a few years, it will surpass even the peak reached in 1929. Low taxes paid by the affluent are only one factor contributing to the great disparity in wealth. The historically high rate of interest, itself the product of wealth concentration, is another.

When the return on investment rises, the rich are the main beneficiaries. Signs of the wealth disparity approaching an all-time high are now everywhere, but its dangers, for lack of proper understanding, are not being recognized. As reported in *The New York Times,* the number of billionaires in the United States nearly doubled in 1986—from fourteen to twenty-six in just one year—thus claiming an increasing share of the nation's wealth at the expense of the poor. The richest 5 percent of Americans have more income than the entire bottom 40 percent. And the richest 1 percent of Americans possess greater wealth than the bottom 90 percent, that is, more than all but 10 percent of the entire population.[27] These are ominous numbers, giving us advance warnings of things to come. A recession is due in 1989–90, and this, combined with a shaky banking system created by the unprecedented concentration of wealth, will give rise to the unprecedented depression of the 1990s.

THE 1920s VS. THE 1980s

We can actually pinpoint 1990 as the year of the world's greatest depression. The analysis in previous chapters demonstrated that the U.S. economy undergoes major cycles every third decade. Since our data are aggregated over a decade, this means that every twenty-nine to thirty-one years a significant transformation occurs in the U.S. economy and society. However, a deeper study of the twentieth-century data reveals that cyclical similarities in the economy are more striking over the sixty-year intervals—twice the length of the three-decade cycle. In this connection let us compare the 1920s with major economic events occurring between 1980 and 1986, the year of the present writing.

First, let us examine general trends; later we will make a year-by-year comparison. We have already seen that the 1920s were marked by low money growth, low inflation, and deregulation. In these respects the 1980s have so far resembled the 1920s. The same holds true with the merger activity among businesses. Both decades reveal a sharp rise in industrial concentration.

The most profitable sector during the 1920s was the automobile industry, which also earned record profits from 1983 to 1986. Reasons for such high earnings, of course, differ between the two decades, but the outcome is nonetheless the same. In general, high-technology industries experienced a sharp growth in the 1920s. The same is true so far in the 1980s.

Banks had mediocre earnings during the 1920s. The same can be said for the first half of the 1980s. Then as now, the farm sector was highly depressed because of the loss of foreign markets and the low prices received by American farmers. Then as now, the coal industry was in the doldrums. So were textiles, shoes, shipping, and railroads, as they are now. Energy prices declined throughout the 1920s. They have done the same so far in the 1980s.

The 1920s were the decade of a Republican presidency with a strikingly pro-business and anti-labor attitude. The 1980s are exactly alike in this respect. Then as now, monetary policy of the Fed reflected Monetarist views. Then as now, eminent economists were convinced that a prolonged depression was impossible, although their logic was totally different. Experts then believed that the capitalist system had an automatic mechanism that tended to cure all its ills, including the problem of unemployment: no help was needed from the government. Today few have faith in that automatic mechanism; rather, the majority opinion now is that the government knows enough to prevent another crisis. Despite major ideological differences, experts are confident that no new great depression is in prospect, just as they were during the 1920s. In fact, two prominent economists of the day, Irving Fisher and Dennis Robertson, gave solemn assurances to the world on the very eve of the economic catastrophe.

There are, of course, some major differences between the decades in question. The government budget showed a surplus during the 1920s, whereas it has shown huge deficits so far in the 1980s and is likely to do so in the foreseeable future. Rates of interest were low at that time; they set new records during the 1980s. The United States in the 1920s enjoyed a large surplus in its balance of trade; it has been suffering unprecedented arrears for the last five years.

These striking disparities between the two decades simply reveal that the West's age of acquisitors, at its zenith during the 1920s, is now gasping for breath. Actually we should not be surprised at the differences, for they are to be expected over time. What is surprising is all the similarities we have detected. And that is where the regular cycles come in.

Let us now turn to a year-by-year comparison. Table 2 shows dramatically how exact the sixty-year cycle can be. The year 1920 experienced high inflation, high unemployment, and high interest rates. Economists of all persuasions, Keynesians, Monetarists, Supply Siders, agree that this is a rare combination—in fact, as rare as a great depression. Yet the same combination occurred sixty years later in 1980. When unemployment increases, aggregate demand goes down, so that businessmen are unable to post big increases in prices. Therefore, high unemployment is usually associated with low inflation, which in turn generates lower interest rates. In other words, high unemployment seldom coexists with high inflation and high rates of interest.

Comparisons of the decade leading up to the Great Depression of the 1930s with the decade of the 80s. All signs indicate that the next three years ('87-'89) will follow the same pattern as the late 20s.

The Six-Decade Cycle: The 1920s vs. the 1980s

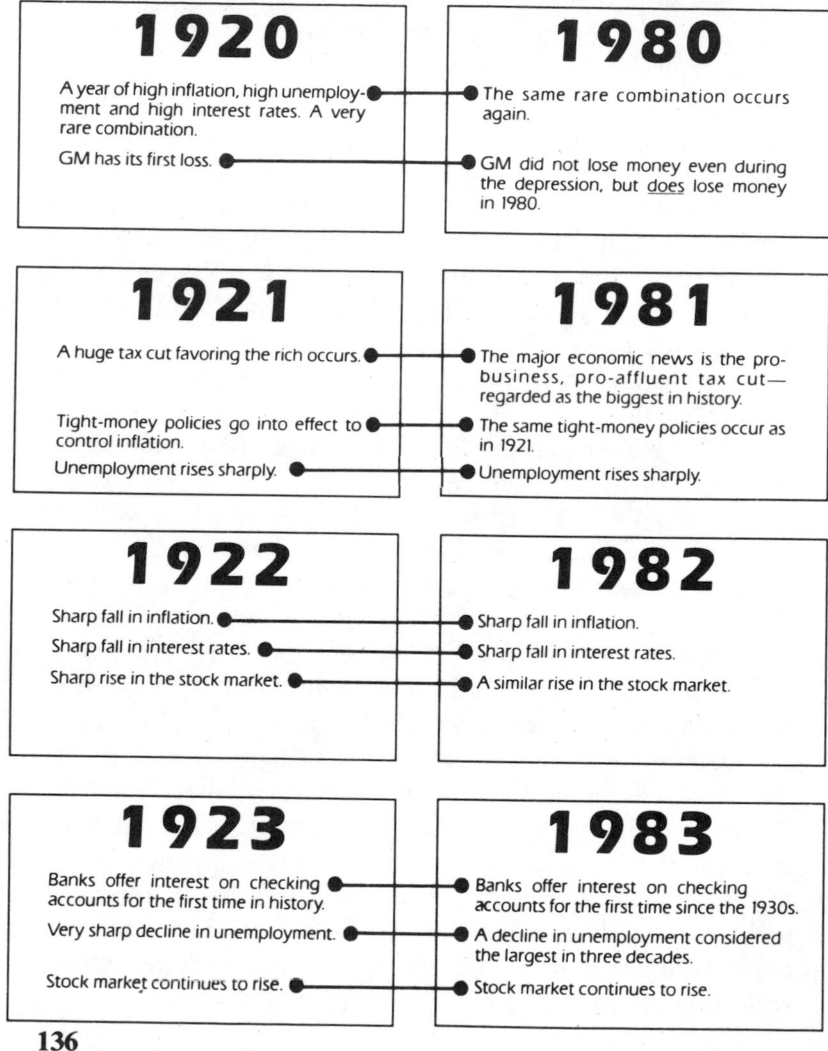

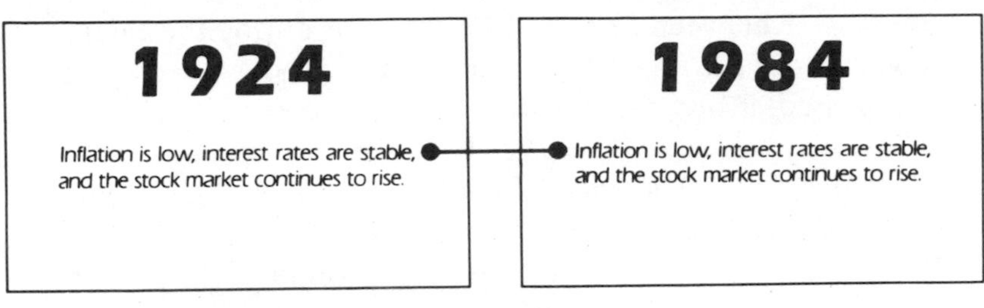

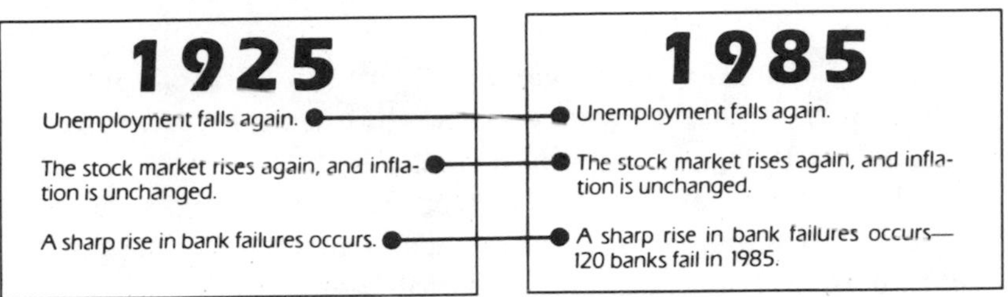

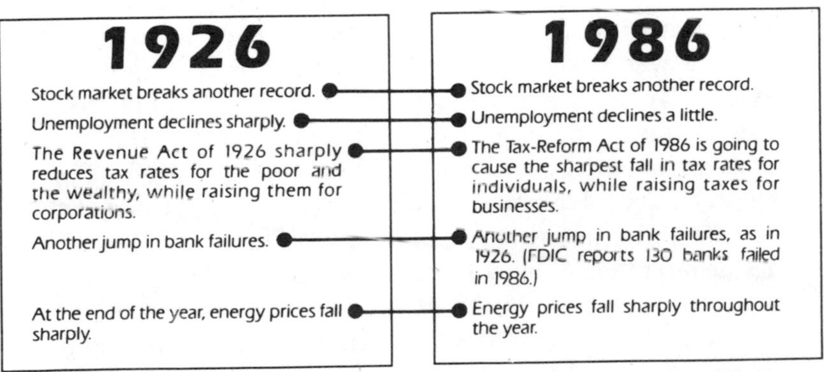

Now let us look at automobile manufacturing, an important sector of the economy. General Motors is the dominant firm in this industry, and in fact there is a saying that what is good for GM is good for America. In 1920 the auto giant had its first loss. It did not lose money again until 1980. This is simply astounding, because the company earned profits every single year between 1921 and 1979—even during the calamitous years of the Great Depression. But as soon as sixty years had passed, it incurred a loss.

The major economic news of 1981 was a tax cut regarded as the biggest in U.S. history. The last time the "biggest" tax cut occurred was in the 1920s, starting with 1921. In both years a Republican president encountered stiff opposition from the Democratic Party to this legislation. Moreover, in both cases the tax cuts favored the rich relative to the poor and the middle class.

In 1921 and 1981 there was a sharp rise in unemployment. Moreover, in both years the rise in unemployment was created by tight-money policies of the Fed.

The highlight of 1982 was a steep decline in interest rates, along with a sharp rise in the stock market. The same occurred in 1922. In addition, inflation slowed down in both years.

The major economic change of 1983 was that banks began to offer interest on checking accounts. The last time this occurred was towards the end of 1923. This is a significant development whose consequences have not been fully recognized. It raises the cost of deposits to the banks, which are then compelled to make risky loans to make a profit. They can no longer let the funds in checking accounts lie idle. This is perhaps the main reason that nowadays we often receive unsolicited offers of bank loans in the mail. This may be a bonanza to borrowers, but it makes the banking system even more fragile, as it did in the 1920s. Congress had outlawed the practice in the 1930s, only to permit the repeat of the error in 1983.

In both 1923 and 1983 the stock market continued to rise. In addition, both years experienced very sharp declines in unemployment.

In 1924 inflation remained low and the stock market continued to rise, while interest rates remained stable. The story in 1984 was much the same.

In 1925 unemployment fell again and the stock market kept rising. The scenario in 1985 was exactly the same.

Energy prices declined sharply in both 1926 and 1986, and so did the rate of inflation, while the stock market registered further gains. Similarly, in both years Congress reduced taxes for individuals and raised them for businesses. In each instance the legislation had rare bipartisan support and won wide approval from the press.

In the first chapter, you will recall, I referred to some forecasts that I made for the U.S. economy in 1984. Now you can see how I was able to foresee economic conditions in 1985 and 1986. Normally the six-decade cycle is not so precise, but for the 1920s and the 1980s it is turning out to be as exact as it possibly can be. In other words, major economic variables in the U.S. economy tend to repeat themselves every six decades, or roughly every fifty-nine to sixty-one years.

We have just seen that many events that occurred between 1980 and 1986 are strikingly similar to those that occurred between 1920 and 1926. Taking the comparison to its logical end, we can look ahead and predict that 1987 will be a year of mediocre growth, as was 1927 at its beginning. But in 1928 the economy expanded briskly and continued to do so until the middle of 1929. Accordingly, we should expect the economy to drift in 1987, grow faster in 1988, and then remain strong until 1989. All this time, inflation will be stable at around 3.5 percent per year, and interest rates, while still historically high, will remain more or less unchanged until 1988 and then rise somewhat in 1989. Energy and farm prices will keep declining relative to other prices.

The stock market will continue to rise, but its total percentage gain by the end of 1987 may not be as strong as its gain in 1986. The market fever will resume in 1988, with occasional retreats and pauses, lasting almost until the end of 1989. Regardless of the stock market behavior, the speculative activity in the options markets will increase sharply for the rest of the 1980s. So will merger activity among industries.

Table 2 implies that, if no remedial measures are taken at this time, then 1989 will be like 1929. This means that at the end of 1989 or in the first half of 1990, the stock market will crash and will be followed by an abysmal decline in business activity and a sharply higher rate of unemployment. The low point of this great depression will come in 1994. The crisis will last at least seven years, from 1990 through 1996.

U.S. Foreign Debt

Is it possible that the depression I forecast simply will not materialize, or that it will remain just a mild recession? Yes, anything is possible; but unless drastic steps are taken now, the likelihood of its occurrence is overwhelming.

In fact, many symptoms of the impending crisis have already appeared. Despite official pronouncements to the contrary, much of the country is already in a recession. In a recent conference, a poll was taken and the governors of thirty-one states said unequivocally that their states were in a slump.[28]

It is also noteworthy that the United States has now become a debtor nation. Foreign debt has piled up at such a breathtaking pace that few are aware of this development, which adds a new dimension to the trouble ahead. In 1985, for the first time in this century, the United States joined the company of nations in hock. By 1986 its foreign debt had reached $250 billion, which exceeded the combined international debt of Mexico and Brazil. The United States now has the dubious distinction of being the largest debtor in the world. In two years it achieved what it took Mexico and Brazil twenty years to achieve.

Actually, the foreign debt situation is worse than it appears. The figure of $250 billion represents the net U.S. indebtedness to the rest of the world. It equals U.S. borrowing minus U.S. lending to other countries, which include many third world nations that are in so much distress themselves that no one expects to receive a penny from them. This is double jeopardy: America is in the position of a person who is up to his ears in debt, yet sees no chance of recovering any of the loans he has made to others.

It should, then, come as no surprise that many banks that lent billions to less developed countries in the 1970s are now facing mounting trouble. Financial institutions that made heavy energy and real estate loans are also close to bankruptcy, because of the collapse in energy prices. In fact, Irvine Sprague, a former board member of the Federal Deposit Insurance Corporation (FDIC), who speaks with the authority of an insider, observes that thousands of banks and savings and loan institutions are now on the government's sick list, and could succumb at any time.[29]

These are all signs of the trouble ahead, and we can ignore them only at our peril.

Before concluding this section, let me try to explain the basic cause of the three-decade and six-decade cycles we have explored. It is very hard to understand why certain events would occur with such regularity. The answer must be sought in the relative constancy of mental and psychological processes. It is human nature alone that can possibly create such cyclical patterns. We usually observe that a generation is active for about thirty years, and then a new one takes over. Every generation finds new ways to make the same mistakes. Apparently the easiest, and relatively painless, way to solve social problems is through government regulation and the printing of money. The temptation of pump-priming is hard to resist. Thus each generation attempts to cure its economic ills through high money growth and regulation. As a result inflation sets in, which eventually invites public outcry. Regulation is then reduced and the money supply tightened, until inflation is brought under control. But two decades later this sequence of events begins again, and the same remedies are applied. Each generation follows in the footsteps of its precursor. Hence the thirty-year cycles.

We all know that war causes suffering. Yet each generation repeats this mistake and goes to war. This is a truism of the way the human mind works. It learns from its own mistakes, but rarely from mistakes made by others.

Some errors, because of their grave consequences, are not repeated in every generation, but in every other generation. In this respect, people repeat not the mistakes of their parents, but of their grandparents. This phenomenon creates the sixty-year cycle. After a large number of fortunes were wiped out in the last depression, for instance, it has taken two generations of inheritance before wealth inequality has reached a critical point again. The ominous impact of this disparity is not recognized by the current generation because the last time that situation arose was sixty years ago.

Whether the mistakes are made by each generation or every other generation determines whether we have a thirty-year or a sixty-year cycle.

International Aspects

The depression of the 1930s was a worldwide event. America, Europe, and the third world were all, one way or another, caught in its throes. In some European countries the crisis had actually begun as early as 1926, although the collapse did not come until after 1929.

While the U.S. economy remained prosperous during much of the 1920s, the British economy was anemic. Britain suffered from severe unemployment throughout the decade, especially after the General Strike of 1926. Many industries, such as coal, steel, shipbuilding, textiles, and housing, were depressed. The rate of unemployment, which was concentrated in Wales and the Northeast, rose to 9.6 percent in 1921, and slowly declined thereafter. In 1926 Britain experienced a severe recession and its GNP declined by more than 4 percent, with unemployment soaring again. The economy recovered somewhat by 1929, but unemployment remained high.

The economic situation in France was much the same. Between 1924 and 1927 the French GNP was stagnant and unemployment reached a new high. Moreover, the franc plummeted because of high government debt. Between 1980 and 1986 French unemployment has hovered around 10 percent and the franc has been under constant pressure, falling to its lowest level in 1984. The British recession of 1926 also spread its tentacles to the French economy, which eventually recovered enough to share the prosperity of the American boom of 1928–29.

The situation in Germany in the 1920s was much worse than in Britain and France. The German economy suffered from hyperinflation caused by the enormous volume of money printed by the government. In 1922 and 1923 the inflation was devastating. The government introduced a new currency in 1923 and also pared its deficit. An international loan in 1924 resulted in much-needed economic stability. But in 1926 unemployment surged to 8 percent. It was not until 1927 that the German economy recovered from the combination of inflation, the resulting financial collapse, and recession.

While Western Europe was in the economic doldrums in the early 1920s, Central Europe fared no better. The Hapsburg Empire was dissolved after the First World War, but the countries that rose from its ruins were too weak to develop viable economies. Both Austria and Hungary were in serious financial trouble right from their birth. It was only after their finances were put under international scrutiny that some degree of stability was achieved. After 1927, however, their economies, fueled by capital inflows from abroad, boomed.

The crux of this whole discussion is that 1926 was a year of serious economic problems in Europe, while the American economy, by and large, managed to avoid the slump. In accordance with the sixty-year cycle, 1986 turned out to be a year of severe recession in Europe, while the U.S. prosperity was more or less unchanged.

Throughout the 1980s, as in the 1920s, Western Europe has suffered from high unemployment. As of 1986 unemployment was 13.4 percent in Britain, 10.5 percent in France, 9 percent in Germany, 12 percent in Belgium, 14.5 percent in Holland, and 20 percent in Spain. The recession of 1986 has created distressful conditions in some countries, especially Britain, France, Holland, and Spain. Between 1987 and 1989 Europe will recover somewhat, but its unemployment problem will remain. When depression afflicts America in 1990, Europe too will suffer in the same proportion, and so will the rest of the world.

Canada is one country whose economy is totally linked with that of the United States. Between 1982 and 1984 unemployment in Canada averaged around 11 percent and, as in the United States, steadily declined afterward. In 1986 it stood at 9.5 percent and is likely to remain at this level. After 1990, however, it will soar to the highest level ever.

Of all the developed economies, Japan has proved the most resilient since the Second World War. Even the oil shocks of 1973 and 1979, when OPEC raised oil prices to new heights, did very little to slow its engine of growth. The Japanese economy adjusts to unexpected pressures much better than any other. This is not surprising, because Japan's age of acquisitors, which began some fifty-five years ago, is very young. It is still in its rising phase in contrast to that in the West. However, in 1990 Japan will face its first sixty-year juncture, or turning point. It will then encounter great difficulties, because its economic health is also linked with the health of the world economy, especially that of the United States.

At this point Japan seems to be in the same position that the United States was in the 1920s. At that time the United States enjoyed a huge trade surplus and was rapidly overtaking Britain as the international financial power. Now Japan, with its more than $80 billion surplus per year, is threatening to surpass the United States. It is already lending huge sums to the world. Moreover, the stock market in Tokyo is currently caught in a greater frenzy than the one in New York. In fact, it is very ominous that the speculative bubble is now building up all over the world. When the bubble bursts, beginning perhaps in Japan, the pain could be far more excruciating than ever before.

In the 1930s the economies of the third world were not as dependent on international commerce as they are today, yet they suffered greatly. This time, however, their suffering will be even greater. Currently, they are benefiting from the huge trade deficits run by the United States each year. But when America sneezes in the 1990s, they will catch pneumonia. The misery I foresee in the cities of India, Mexico, Brazil, Pakistan, Egypt, and the rest of the third world is beyond my powers of description.

International economic ills of the 1980s are reminiscent of those of the 1920s, but their dimensions have grown drastically. The main threat to the world economy today springs from the huge international debt of the third world and the rising chorus of protectionism in America. The debt problem resembles the problem of war reparations facing Germany and its trading partners, especially France, during the 1920s.

However, the international debt load today is much heavier and afflicts many more countries than in the past. The war reparations problem pales before the current affliction of world debt.

The threat to international stability stemming from growing protectionist demands in the United States had a parallel in the 1920s, but at that time the foreign-trade sector was small relative to the rest of the American economy. Now the share of exports in the U.S. GNP has more than doubled, and if the government gives in to protectionist pressures the potential for damage is much greater today than ever before.

Protectionism means reducing foreign access to domestic markets. When one country creates such barriers, others usually follow suit, so that there is a general contraction in international trade, resulting in diminished business activity everywhere. The world is much more interdependent today than in the past. Hence, protectionist pressures should be resisted at all costs. If not, the worldwide depression will be much deeper than otherwise.

The diminution of world trade, however, may be unavoidable. Trade requires credit, which, because of colossal foreign debts, is growing scarce. A time might come when banks refuse all lending to debtor countries. That will then precipitate a crisis and eventually a worldwide depression.

8

STRATEGY FOR INVESTMENT

I HAVE BEEN arguing that, given government mismanagement and the misguided fiscal policies of the 1980s, the depression of 1990 is now all but inevitable. The supporting evidence for this conclusion comes from a wide spectrum of sources, including the long-run patterns of money growth, inflation, regulation, and depressions, and above all, the law of social cycles.

What can we do now to prepare for this eventuality? The year 1990 is rapidly approaching, but there is still time for defensive action before we are hit by the calamity.

There is a story in the Old Testament in which Joseph interprets the Pharaoh's dream, saying that there will be seven years of plenty followed by seven years of famine. He goes on to advise the Pharaoh to store food and grain from his surplus and take other steps in preparation for the impending catastrophe. This biblical parable is no less relevant today, for all the evidence shows that there will be seven years of prosperity between 1983 and 1989, followed by seven years of economic drought from 1990 through 1996.

Now let's explore just how that drought will manifest itself.

INFLATIONARY DEPRESSION

One question that comes up each time there is talk of depression is whether the next one will be inflationary or deflationary. Will it be like the hyperinflationary whirlwind in Germany in 1923 or like the deflationary collapse in the United States in the 1930s?

There are strong arguments on both sides of the question. Some suggest that the government would never allow the repeat of a 1929-style tragedy. If there was a run on the banks in the future, the government would quickly come to their rescue; similarly, the government would not raise taxes again in the midst of a recession even if the budget deficit soared still higher. Of course, the government might then have to print billions and billions of dollars of additional money, but it would not stand idly by if the panic-stricken public began to withdraw its funds from the banks. If that happened, then the depression would be accompanied by soaring inflation.

The other side of the argument is that potential problems of the private bond, credit, and stock markets are still far greater than the size of the government debt. In a crisis initiated by, say, a stock market crash, there would be such an erosion of confidence in the economy that investment, consumption, and world trade would drastically decline, so that the government's efforts to stimulate the economy through extraordinary increases in money supply would not be enough to prevent a collapse in commodity prices. In this scenario, then, the coming depression would be deflationary, one in which a dramatic decline in business activity generates an equally dramatic fall in prices.

There could also be a third eventuality. It need not necessarily be a deflationary or an inflationary situation. We could simply have price stability, with a slight downward trend. Prices on the average could fall about 10 percent over seven years between 1990 through 1996.

The historical record, of course, points toward a deflationary depression. This country has never, in all its history, had an inflationary depression. Yet whenever business falters nowadays, the government's first recourse is to raise the budget deficit and increase the growth of money. We have been addicted to policies of easy money and credit for a long time and are not likely to abandon them in the near future.

However, the memory of the double-digit inflation through much of the 1970s and all the way up to 1981 is still fresh in our minds. The government is therefore unlikely to unleash the engines of money growth, at least in the near future. The more likely policy in any crisis would be a relatively restrained expansion of money growth. This, coupled with deflationary pressures stemming from the private-sector depression, could lead to more or less stable prices in the 1990s, with a slightly downward bias.

This scenario is also compatible with the three-decade cycle of inflation, in which the 1970s were the last peak decade of inflation. According to this pattern, we are not due for another bout of inflation until the first decade of the next century. For all these reasons, it seems unlikely that inflation will return in the near future. If anything, prices, especially at the wholesale level, could actually fall in the 1990s.

Overall, then, the cost of living will be more or less stable in the 1990s, but it will seem like deflation compared to the rising prices of the 1980s. We may call it relative deflation, which will cause a further decline in interest rates. This is because interest rates and inflation tend to rise and fall together, just as they did during the 1970s and 1980s.

In spite of overall price stability, some product prices will fall sharply. Luxury items and real estate, being expensive, are subject to greater price fluctuations than the necessities, at least in absolute terms. When the depression comes, these items, along with oil, raw materials, and farm products will experience a serious deflation, while the cost of services will probably keep rising.

These considerations have an important bearing on any steps we can now take to meet the impending crisis, for it is necessary to know what prices and interest rates are likely to do in the future.

Obviously your savings and investment strategy will vary according to your income, assets, and appetite for risk. Some of you may be extremely rich, others comfortably middle class, and some of you may be struggling to stay afloat. Some of you may hope to profit from the coming depression, while others will be happy just to survive it without undue hardship. But regardless of your income and wealth bracket, some investments should be avoided by everybody; others are in everyone's interest, and still others are not for the faint-hearted.

I personally try to avoid risky investments, but you may have different goals and preferences. I will simply give you the pros and cons of various options and, at the end of this chapter, design a conservative, defensive strategy that, while it will not make you a multimillionaire, will protect you from a very real threat during a depression—that of personal bankruptcy.

HOW MUCH SHOULD I SAVE?

Remember that during a depression unemployment rises drastically and earnings of the employed fall sharply. Fortunately, the economy will be fairly prosperous right up until 1989. Therefore, you should begin to increase your savings now, avoiding frivolous and unnecessary purchases. Spending on luxuries should be greatly reduced, and whenever possible, eliminated. This may sound like an austere regimen, but believe me, it will pay off later. Think of it this way: Even if you have no faith in my words and seriously doubt the possibility of another depression, the strategy of increasing your savings cannot hurt. You'll increase your cash reserves, and of course you can always buy things later. (In this regard, you might bear in mind Thoreau's observation, "A man is rich in proportion to what he can do without.")

How much money should you try to save between now and 1990? Assuming the worst-case scenario, where a person loses his job and has to live totally on his assets, a family of four on an austerity budget would need about $11,000 per year to survive the depression. That is where the official poverty line begins at today's price levels, which are unlikely to be very different in the 1990s. If the person remains unemployed for, say, four years, obviously savings of about $44,000 will be needed to live through the worst of the crisis. That will be enough to buy subsistence. However, for a family of four living in a major urban center, such as New York, San Francisco, Los Angeles, Boston, or Chicago, $20,000 per year would be more realistic.

Social Security and Private Pensions

Those of you living on fixed incomes from Social Security and pensions should be aware of special risks. During the 1990s, as tax receipts decline with the economy, the budget deficit will rise to dizzying heights. While Congress will try its best to maintain the Social Security system, it may have no choice but to trim the payments. Government pensions could meet a similar fate. Therefore, all of us, whether retired or not, should try to raise our current rate of savings.

What about private pensions, i.e., employee pension plans that have been invested in a variety of financial instruments, such as stocks, bonds, and real estate, among others? Thousands of businesses are going to fail in the coming depression; thousands of others will survive, but we don't know which ones. In an extended depression, some of the pension funds, which depend on the health of the industries in which they are invested, could also go bankrupt. You could then be left with a worthless piece of paper. If you have a choice to take out your pension in a lump sum or in the form of an annuity spread over several years, you should take it all or as much as possible before 1990.

Some private pensions are insured by the government. When businesses fail, these pension liabilities become a federal responsibility. But don't count on it. How many problems can the government tackle at the same time? It provides insurance for bank deposits of up to $100,000; it insures residential mortgages, pensions, and farm loans. Above all, it has an annual budget deficit of $200 billion year after year. We can't depend on the government to cure all our ills. Clearly, we have to take action on our own before 1990, and withdraw as much of our money from pension funds as possible.

KEOGH PLANS AND IRAs

The same goes for Keogh plans and IRAs. A few years ago Congress created two new tax-deferred devices—the Keogh plan for the self-employed, and the Individual Retirement Account (IRA) for others earning up to $40,000. With these vehicles a qualified person can reduce his taxable income by certain amounts, which must be set aside with an approved trustee. This tax-deferred fund can grow until you are fifty-nine and a half, when you can withdraw your money either in a lump sum or in the form of a yearly annuity. Of course, you have to pay the tax at the time of withdrawal.

If you will be fifty-nine and a half before 1990, then the decision about your Keogh or IRA plan is very simple. Just take it all out in a lump sum. The tax consequences are minor with this decision, because under the Tax Reform Act of 1986 you will be either in the 15 percent income tax bracket or the 28 percent bracket, but no more than that. However, if you are not fifty-nine and a half by 1990, then the decision becomes complicated, because there are penalties for premature withdrawal. The tax penalty is 10 percent of the amount withdrawn. In addition, the trustee may impose a penalty of its own.

The decision ultimately depends on the safety of the vehicles in which the Keogh or IRA funds are invested. Banks are safer than many brokerage houses, because bank deposits as well as these plans are each insured for up to $100,000 by the government. In any coming crisis the government's first priority will be the solvency of financial institutions. The FDIC (Federal Deposit Insurance Corporation) and the FSLIC (Federal Savings and Loan Insurance Corporation) will try their best to keep the banks afloat and protect up to $100,000 of each deposit, even if billions of dollars of new money have to be printed. But there is also the threat of hyperinflation resulting from inordinate monetary expansion. In a crunch, the government may decide to honor only a part of its commitments to the depositors; for example, a limit of only $50,000 might be set.

Premature withdrawal of funds in Keogh and IRA plans may then be the safest bet in spite of various penalties, especially if they are entrusted to non-banking institutions. The next question is: What should you do with the money? Can you trust the banks at all?

In spite of many safeguards provided by the government, hundreds of banks have failed in the 1980s, and thousands more will fail in the 1990s. In fact, there were more bank failures in 1985 and 1986 than at any time since the 1930s. Yet the depositors have been fully protected so far. They may have faced no more than minor inconvenience. However, as I said above, during the depression the government may decide to honor only a part of its commitments.

Even if the government fully protects the depositors from bank failures, there are bound to be delays and inconveniences in the case of a major crisis. Remember what happened to the troubled savings institutions in Ohio and Maryland in 1985, where for a while depositors were allowed to withdraw only $1,000 from their accounts. A reasonable strategy for the safekeeping of your money, then, is to keep only a third of it in a bank account, a third in a safe-deposit box, and another third at home, beginning in 1990. All cash in your safe-deposit box is yours, and even a bankrupt bank can't legally deny you access to it.

How Should I Invest My Savings?

Once you have decided to increase the amount of your savings, you need proper investment vehicles for their growth. A bewildering variety of such vehicles is available nowadays, from money market funds to commodity futures and options. I am not going to lead you to the latter, because even many experts suffer huge losses in these volatile markets. Of course, there are always a lucky few who become rich in a hurry, but the likelihood for you and me to join their ranks is very small.

A safe investment strategy, then, is one that yields a reasonable return without unduly endangering the investment itself. A number of options are available in this regard, but before I make specific recommendations, let's review the pros and cons of various investment devices.

Real Estate

Real estate was the darling of investors in the 1970s as speculation and double-digit inflation dramatically raised the prices of houses, apartments, and office buildings. Some people earned huge profits, and a few became millionaires overnight. However, the real estate investment boom has come and gone, and you should not expect the dramatic rise in value we saw in the 1970s. This is because inflation has gradually declined during the 1980s, and even though interest rates have also fallen, in many parts of the country it is more difficult to sell a house today than just a few years ago.

Plainly speaking, real estate will be a bad investment during the rest of the 1980s and will become desirable in the 1990s only after prices have radically declined. (The hardest-hit areas will be small towns and small to midsize cities.) The housing market has generally shrunk, whereas commercial real estate has simply collapsed in many areas, not only in the Oil Belt states but also in parts of the West, Rocky Mountains, Midwest, and Southeast. According to *The Wall Street Journal,* "In some cases, the deflation in commercial property is worse than that during the Depression, when values fell, on the average, by roughly one-third."[30]

It used to be that real estate was a great tax shelter. But the tax reforms of 1986 have changed all that, greatly reducing depreciation expense and limiting your ability to write off losses against other income. Hence from the tax angle also, you should avoid real estate investments. Even owning your own home has fewer tax advantages, because of the reduction in the tax brackets.

If you don't own a house already, then don't buy one, at least not for investment purposes. Renting today is more prudent than buying, because rents in many areas are less than monthly mortgage payments. If you insist on owning rather than renting, then buy an inexpensive residence and finance it through a variable-rate mortgage rather than a fixed-rate mortgage. Even though interest rates have generally declined, mortgage rates are still hovering around 10 percent. I expect them to remain stable until 1988, rise a bit in 1989, and then fall sharply in the 1990s. In any case, your down payment should be as low as possible, because staying liquid with cash is the key to surviving a depression.

Should you sell your house between now and 1989? The very thought of this will be intolerable to many readers. The answer depends on how emotionally attached you are to your homestead, and the size of your monthly mortgage. Since house prices are likely to fall sharply in the 1990s, strictly financial considerations would dictate the sale of your residence before the end of 1989. But moving from a house to an apartment is likely to be disruptive. You may have to give up a lot of comforts, your children may hate moving to a new neighborhood and schools, and so on. This is therefore a decision you will have to weigh carefully.

However, if your mortgage payment is too high and eating up a big chunk of your earnings, leaving little for savings, then you should sell your residence as soon as possible. Saving money at this time, in my view, takes priority over the comforts and amenities of owning one's home. Timely action of this type could save you from personal bankruptcy in the future.

If you cannot bring yourself to sell your home, you should refinance a fixed-rate mortgage into a variable-rate mortgage by the end of 1989, when the banks will still be hungry for new business and your credit rating will still be high. During the 1990s who knows if you and I will have a job?

Of course, it is possible for a homeowner to sell his or her house and still inhabit it, by selling it to an investor and then leasing it back. Another alternative that can be very attractive to older people living on a fixed income is equity sharing. Under this plan an investor becomes, in effect, co-owner of your house, assuming the burden of your mortgage payments and thus allowing you to live in your home rent-free. At your death, or after an agreed-upon number of years, the co-owner has the right to sell the property.

If the homeowner has a difficult choice to make, the strategy for the investor is very clear. If you own investment properties in residential real estate, you should plan on selling between now and 1989, take your profits, and then be well positioned to buy properties in the 1990s, possibly for as little as one-half their current selling prices.

Stocks

Between 1987 and 1989 the performance of the economy will be more or less mediocre, but the stock market will keep rising, especially in 1988 and 1989. For one thing, wealth disparity is now growing at a fast pace, and when too few people have too much wealth, financial markets tend to boom. For another, the Tax Reform Act of 1986 is bullish for stocks, because they will attract much of the wealth previously invested in real estate. With real estate shelters declining in profitability and with inflation under control, stocks will be a better place to invest your money than any other financial instrument.

You have two basic ways to pick stocks. One way is simply to pick them yourself, and the other is to let the experts—stockbrokers or managers of mutual funds—choose them for you. It is true that even the experts go wrong. However, in a bull market, where the downside risk is rather low, you should invest in blue-chip stocks and hold on to them. Where the average investor gets into trouble is in trying to outguess the market, continually trading, buying and selling short-term, rather than "hanging in there" and riding with the upward trend of the market. Just don't get into anything that carries a high degree of risk and avoid stocks in industries that have fallen on hard times. Oil stocks and stocks dealing with the construction industry are examples of today's losers. Blue chips, however, will keep rising, and many growth stocks will outperform the market average.

If you don't want to use a broker or pick stocks yourself, your best bet may be to buy no-load or low-load mutual funds investing in growth stocks. Such funds are run by savvy managers, and the no-load funds do not charge a fee. They are listed daily in *The Wall Street Journal;* look for the initials "N.L." (no-load) next to the fund's price. Magazines like *Money* and *Kiplinger's* periodically rate the ten-year and five-year performance of mutual fund groups.

Unless you have had great success with stocks in the past, I don't advise you to pick them on your own. Recently a Dallas newspaper held a stock-picking contest in which an elderly woman won. Others who were presumably well versed in stock market dealings lost out to someone who had picked only stocks she had heard of. There is no foolproof theory of how to buy securities. Brokerage firms with up-to-date information, however, can usually keep you away from obvious losers. In a bull market, you can't lose with a large majority of stocks, provided you hold them long enough.

Bonds

Bonds are not as risky as stocks, but their potential for appreciation is limited. Bond prices decline when interest rates go up and rise when interest rates fall. In 1984 I advised my readers to buy long-term bonds. Those of you who did must have realized great appreciation in your portfolios by now. The same cannot be said for bonds bought between now and 1989, because interest rates are unlikely to decline any further in that time. They will rise somewhat in 1989 before falling again in the 1990s. There is not much downside risk in their price, at least in the next two years. And they should be part of any diversified portfolio.

Bonds were a poor investment during the 1970s, which was the latest peak decade of the long-run cycle of inflation. As a result, interest rates rose to the stratosphere and bond prices fell into a bottomless pit. However, in the next fifteen years the risk of persistent inflation is very small. Bonds could then turn out to be great assets, provided their issuers do not default. This is a big proviso, and it applies to almost all investments after 1989. I will have more to say about this later in the chapter.

Most people purchase bonds for income and safety. Obviously, U.S. Treasury bonds are the safest, but their return is commensurately low. Next in safety are the AAA corporate bonds, with slightly higher interest rates. In general, the lower the rating, the higher the return. A good mix of safety and return is in A-rated corporate bonds, which are reasonably safe and yield modest interest as well.

Municipal bonds with an A or better rating are also relatively safe; they are tax-free as well. But the 1986 tax act has reduced the allure of their tax-free status, since the top tax rates will be cut to 28 percent by 1988. Moreover, we should remember that in a depression many municipalities also default. Only U.S. Treasury bonds may be worth keeping at that time.

Convertible bonds have a lower yield than the nonconvertible bonds discussed above, but their potential for appreciation is higher because they are exchangeable into a certain fixed amount of the issuer's common stock. They offer a guaranteed return, and, being linked to the underlying stock because of their convertibility, if the price of the stock goes up, the value of the bond increases. For those who dislike the low dividends generally paid by common stocks and yet would like to participate in the coming stock market boom, convertible bonds offer an excellent option. They are a hybrid between a stock and a bond, and they have the best risk/reward combination of any security.

Money Market Accounts

Money market accounts are offered by banks as a place where you can park your funds temporarily. MMAs are the banks' answer to MMFs (money market funds), which are generally offered by brokerage houses. Both MMAs and MMFs are highly liquid vehicles, and their yields are slightly higher than those of the short-term U.S. Treasury bills. However, MMAs are insured by the FDIC up to $100,000, and thus are preferable to MMFs. In any case, you should place your funds in these vehicles only as a resting place until you are ready to make your next investment.

Gold Coins

Precious metals, such as gold, silver, and platinum, are among the riskiest investments, but they often do very well in an inflationary economy. Those who believe inflation will accelerate in the future suggest that we put a large portion of our funds in precious metals—"Go with the glitter."

Gold experienced two great bull markets in the 1970s, increasing dramatically from $35 in 1971 to $200 in 1974. It then dropped to a low of $103 in 1976, after which it soared to an astonishing high of $886 in 1980. But aside from the professionals who make a living touting the virtues of gold (known as the "hard-money" gang), very few general money advisers foresee gold as a major growth area. My own belief is that the professional gold hucksters have made a lot of money for themselves selling their advice to others but not much for their clients.

Gold as an investment is not a good choice for us ordinary folks. Those who have strong stomachs or a lot of money to burn can gamble with precious metals, but unless you are highly sophisticated in this area and can spend every day charting their performance, don't get involved. Gold can rise and fall so fast that the timing of buying and selling is of utmost importance. But there are very few with such an astute sense of timing. By "gold" I am referring specifically to gold bullion or coins. I don't recommend them as an investment for the common man.

But gold as a hedge against calamity is something else. Whenever times are tumultuous, people turn to gold. This is the dictum of ten thousand years of human history, and has been true in every society since man turned from barter to gold as a medium of exchange. Currencies may come and go, but gold retains its eternal luster.

Precious metals tend to appreciate in value during inflation, and depreciate during disinflation or outright deflation. Ordinarily, I would not recommend the purchase of gold now or in the future, because of the impending threat of relative deflation. I expect prices to be more or less stable in the coming depression. But the 1990s are not going to be ordinary times. Throughout history, people have turned to gold during uncertain periods. But the uncertainty has to be dire; it has to last for a long time, and it has to create massive social unrest before people will abandon their currency en masse and turn to precious metals. Something like this could happen in the 1990s as the age of acquisitors comes to an end.

But it should be clear that I do not recommend gold as a speculative investment. It is worth considering only as insurance against a financial collapse. No matter what happens to the value of the dollar if the government attempts to stimulate the economy in the 1990s by pouring enormous amounts of new money into circulation, gold will hold its value.

Gold, by itself, does not yield any return. No one pays you interest when you park your funds in precious metals. Gold, of course, can appreciate—and fast; but it can also depreciate fast.

Between gold bullion and coins, I prefer the coins. They do cost a bit more than bullion, but they have higher liquidity and some of them are also legal tender, that is, you can use them as currency in the country issuing them. There are many countries offering gold coins today. Mexico, Canada, South Africa, Austria, and Hungary have minted them for years. In addition, the United States, Australia, and Japan introduced their own coins at the end of 1986.

For U.S. investors, the best coin may be the American Eagle, which is available in four sizes—one ounce, half-ounce, quarter-ounce, and one-tenth ounce. Like the South African Krugerrand, it is 91.67 percent pure gold; it has lower gold content than the Canadian Maple Leaf, which is 99.99 percent pure. Some people prefer the Canadian coin because of its purity, others the Krugerrand because of its longevity, but the American coin is likely to dominate this market in the near future.

The U.S. coin's status as legal tender might exempt it from sales tax in some states. National pride could also make it attractive to U.S. investors, although currently the Maple Leaf is the most popular among all the coins. The Krugerrand is the most widely held coin in the world, but apartheid troubles in South Africa have been hurting its popularity in the 1980s. (These coins are not the same as numismatic coins, which are collector's items valued more for their scarcity and antiquity than for their gold content.)

You can buy gold coins from a number of dealers. Pay cash only upon delivery. If you are ordering by mail, use a "sight draft" through a bank. The coins are then shipped to that bank, and the bank simultaneously releases the coins to you and the money to the dealer. If convenient, you should store your coins in a safe-deposit box at the same bank.

Many jewelry stores also deal in coins. Look in the Yellow Pages under the heading "Gold Dealers."

Gold Stocks

Another way to participate in the glitter of gold is to buy shares of companies involved in gold-mining operations. Many such companies are located in South Africa, which is currently in great social and economic turmoil. These shares, of course, should be avoided. A better choice would be non-African gold companies such as Campbell Red Lake, Homestake, and Dome Mining, traded on the New York Stock Exchange, or Echo Bay and Giant Yellowknife, traded on the American Exchange. However, in the coming bull market, 1987–89, gold stocks will consistently lag behind other securities.

Silver Coins

Prices of all precious metals usually move together. When gold goes up, so does silver, and vice versa. Deflation is bad for both silver and gold, whereas uncertainty and social unrest benefit both. Silver, however, is much more affordable than gold, and may have a larger market. It is also bulkier and harder to store than gold. In my view gold is preferable to silver as a hedge against calamity, but if you can't afford the yellow metal, it's worth considering silver.

Silver bullion or silver coins can be bought from the same dealers handling gold coins. Here again, the same caution should be exercised as in the purchase and storage of gold.

Just as silver is more affordable than gold, so are silver mining shares. But silver mines are not financially as strong as gold mines. And in a bear market they may have great trouble staying in business or maintaining their dividends. If you wish to pursue this investment area, some of the more notable of the silver companies are ASARCO, Inc., Gold Resources and Chemical Corporation, Homestake Mining Company, Phelps-Dodge Corporation, and Silver King.

Silver is mostly a byproduct in the extraction of other metals, especially copper. During recessions and depressions prices of nonprecious metals fall drastically. For that reason alone silver shares should be avoided, since metal prices have recently been falling, and in the future will fall even more.

Stock Options

A stock option gives an investor the right to buy or sell shares at a given price on or before some future date. A smart investor can use it to increase his income and at the same time limit his risk from the purchase of shares. His maximum loss is the price he paid for the option, but his gain can be several times the purchase price.

Options are listed on the business pages of most major newspapers as well as in *The Wall Street Journal.* The right to buy a number of shares on or before a certain date at a certain price is called a "call" option, and the right to sell a number of shares on or before a certain date at a certain price is called a "put" option. If you expect a stock to appreciate, you should buy a call option, and if you expect it to depreciate, you should buy a put option. In either case, your maximum loss is the price you pay for the option.

However, the option price itself is determined by the market. It moves much more rapidly than the price of the stock it represents. Some people simply bet on the option price itself, hoping it will go up. They have no desire to buy or sell the stock at the specified price.

YOUR BEST INVESTMENT STRATEGY

By now you have seen that a wide variety of options is available to you. The real question is what your investment strategy should be between now and 1990. How should you allocate your savings into MMAs, bonds, stocks, real estate, gold, and other precious metals?

I suggested earlier that a four-year total of $44,000 is the absolute minimum that a family of four will need in the coming crisis. This is your survival insurance. If your savings or assets that can be turned into cash are below this amount, don't take any kind of investment risk. Just put your money in a money market account and let it earn the low interest. True, there are far better rates of return from other investments, but you can't take a chance with your survival money. If your circumstances are limited, at most you should place these funds in U.S. Treasury or AAA corporate bonds.

For those of you who have funds beyond the bare minimum needed for survival, you will have to invest these extra or surplus savings carefully. You should avoid real estate as an investment for the reasons previously explained. If you insist on buying a house, go with a variable-rate mortgage, but don't expect much appreciation in the value of your home. In fact, be prepared for a large depreciation in the 1990s. The virtue of the variable-rate mortgage is that your monthly payment will also go down sharply. We are now, and have been for the last four years, in the declining phase of the long-run cycle of inflation, and under such conditions real estate is not a good investment for your savings.

If you dislike risk, you can put your extra savings into U.S. Treasury bonds or AAA-rated corporate bonds. If you are a slight risk-taker, you might buy A-rated bonds, or convertible bonds of some blue-chip companies or even of companies regarded as growth stocks. Avoid precious metals at this time. The world is not on fire at present; nor do I expect inflation to return and persist. Hold off investing in gold or silver until the end of the decade.

If you are a risk-taker, then there are much better alternatives waiting for you in the financial markets. I would suggest you put a part of your extra savings into growth mutual funds, preferably of the no-load variety. If you purchase shares, then sell call options to limit your risk and enhance your income.

Finally, there is a diversified portfolio, which combines the good points of all the investment vehicles just described. This portfolio should have a minimum of $44,000 in MMAs or other bank accounts, 25 percent of your surplus savings in bonds, 25 percent in mutual funds, and the remainder divided evenly between convertible bonds and stocks.

The stock market rise has not run its full course yet. While 1987 will be a strong year, 1988, after a correction in first quarter, will be a real boom period, which could continue into 1989.

As for gold, we know it is not a good asset in disinflationary times, but its value usually rises during a crisis. Gold yields no return, while stocks, bonds, and MMAs do. Since the economy will be relatively prosperous until 1989, the purchase of gold as a safe haven is not advisable until then, unless its price comes down from its late 1986 range of $400 an ounce to about $300.

After June 1989, you should slowly start selling your convertible bonds, mutual funds, and stocks. The market is likely to crash toward the end of 1989 or in the first quarter of 1990. Obviously nobody wants this to happen, and if somehow we are fortunate and there is no crash, then you should continue to hold your nonconvertible bonds. In the meantime, invest the proceeds from your liquidated assets in MMAs, deposited in more than one bank for safety, and keep some cash in a safe-deposit box and at home.

If the market indeed crashes, then for certain a depression is coming. Start buying gold and silver coins at that time; you might also purchase some gold shares. Simultaneously, start selling your corporate bonds and keep only the U.S. Treasury bonds. After 1991 you should get rid of even these bonds and hold on to cash or gold.

In short, you should start selling your assets linked to common stocks after mid-1989, and then adopt a wait-and-see attitude for your cash and remaining assets. The decisions about your IRA, Keogh plan, and other pension options should be postponed until the collapse of the stock market. But take action at the very first sign of the crash. The last quarter of 1989 and the first quarter of 1990 are the crucial months to watch. If the stock market drops no more than 20 percent during these six months, then the biggest danger has been perhaps averted. The depression could just turn out to be no more than a serious recession, which does not call for such drastic action as the cashing-in of IRAs and Keogh plans, hoarding gold, and so on.

The next point to watch in the 1990s would be the last quarter of 1993 and the first half of 1994. Based on the six-decade cycle, the next depression could occur at any time in the first half of the 1990s. If the first two years of the decade escape economic calamity, then watch out for 1993–94. If the stock market still fails to crash and the depression fails to materialize, then the danger for all practical purposes will have passed.

Advice for Businessmen

The advice I have just given holds good for all people, rich and poor, young and old, married and unmarried. For businessmen I have a few other suggestions as well.

First, try to reduce your debt as much as possible by the end of 1989, or convert your short-term loans into long-term debt. Assumption of debt to finance company growth is a good strategy during times of inflation, but disinflation or relative deflation are very hard on debtors.

Second, avoid investments with a long gestation period. Despite the traditional virtues of long-term planning, for the time being think short. In other words, you shouldn't begin projects that will pay off in the 1990s. If you must start a long-term project, use your own company's resources and cash. Heavy indebtedness could result in bankruptcy.

Third, if at all possible, diversify into a repair-type business, which has a better survival chance in a depression than many other businesses. People will not have the money to buy new houses, cars, or appliances. They will simply keep them longer and put more money into repair and maintenance. Service businesses will also do better than manufacturing and high-tech companies.

The general advice I have just given to businessmen applies especially to small businesses, which are often undercapitalized, pay more for bank loans, and lack the reserves to carry them through an extended depression. Small business proprietors should make every effort to be completely out of debt by the end of 1989. If you own a small business, stay away from ambitious projects involving heavy investment at this time. Put your funds in the stock market instead, where you can still earn a fairly high return.

If your lease is up for renewal, try to get a short-term lease so that you are not locked into a long-term, high-rent obligation. Rents are likely to decline sharply in the 1990s. If you are unable to obtain a short-term lease, or would like the peace of mind that comes with a long-term contract, try to have your rent linked to the rate of inflation. The risk of high inflation is minimal in the 1990s; the probability of a downward trend is high.

Low overhead costs and inventory control are the keys to success in a small business. A large concern can afford to ignore these savings, but not a venture of modest size. Inventory control will be especially important in 1990 and thereafter. It is crucial that you not get stuck with excessive levels of unsold goods, which could lead to insolvency.

SUMMARY

To summarize, here are the various steps you need to take between now and the end of 1989.

1. Spend less and save more.
2. Reduce your debt as much as possible.
3. Between now and 1989, invest in bonds, stocks, and mutual funds.
4. Avoid real estate investments and, until 1989, gold, unless its price falls close to $300 per ounce.
5. Sell all stocks and stock-related assets and real estate after the middle of 1989, but keep U.S. Treasury bonds and AAA corporate bonds.
6. If, after late 1989, the stock market crashes, immediately cash in your IRAs, Keogh plans, and, if possible, other

pension programs regardless of any penalties for premature withdrawal.

7. Then start buying gold and silver coins and, possibly, gold shares.

8. After 1991, if the depression has already taken hold, get in the maximum survival position; namely, hold only cash and precious metals, kept partly at home and partly in a safe-deposit box.

9

HOW CAN WE PREVENT ANOTHER DEPRESSION?

I AM PERHAPS the only forecaster in history who fervently hopes that his prophecies turn out to be totally wrong. I have given you a long list of do's and don'ts in the previous chapter, and I earnestly hope that these defensive measures to prepare for the Great Depression of 1990 will prove unwarranted. Let's try to make sure, individually and collectively, that there is no future crisis. "An ounce of prevention is worth a pound of cure" might be a cliché, but we need to believe in it now as never before. Is it possible, then, to avert or at least minimize the next depression, which could be more cataclysmic than any mankind has yet seen?

Napoleon was fond of saying that the word "impossible" exists only in the dictionary of fools. That is my sentiment as well. As we have seen, all historical patterns point toward the inevitability of a depression in the 1990s. But every event has a cause. The seeds of a new depression have already been sown by the Reagan Administration. Yet it is not altogether too late. Steps can still be taken to blunt the impending crisis. The challenge is formidable, and the timetable all too short. But to recognize the problem and do nothing is to court defeat—both as individuals and as a nation.

Clearly, the solution lies not in short-term fixes, but in fundamental reforms which go to the very root of our economic ills. Many times before, the economy has been in tumult which led to perfunctory changes that merely cured the symptoms but not the cause. One looks in vain over the nation's past to find any truly fundamental economic reforms in the face of massive upheaval. Every crisis has resulted in the creation of some institutions which solved the problem in the short run, but created new and more serious ills in the long run. Thus the national currency system was born in the 1860s, the Federal Reserve System in the 1910s, the New Deal in the 1930s. The problems they addressed vanished temporarily, only to return with a vengeance. Reforms are needed again, yet I fear that countervailing political realities make it unlikely that anything will really be done to avert the crisis.

Logic of Reforms

Historically, the periodic reforms introduced in the American economy have been superficial in nature. Let us see what such changes are bound to do. Consider Chart 10, which plots time along the horizontal axis and the evolution of any entity along the vertical axis. The diagram illustrates the time path of any social phenomenon. As we noted earlier, nothing moves in a straight line, regardless of the direction of the trend. All things evolve in cycles. When the trend is upward, each peak is higher than the preceding peak; and when the trend is downward, each successive trough is lower than the

Chart 10 / **Impact of Superficial Reforms**

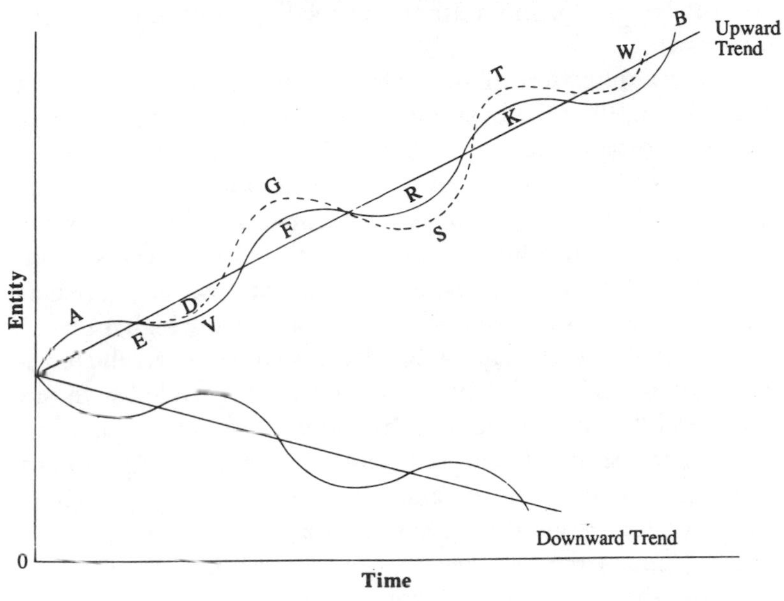

one before it. This is how everything behaves over time—in up-and-down patterns, which may be regular or irregular.

Every entity has its own momentum and a cyclical pattern of varying duration. Sometimes it is in the upswing; at other times, in the downswing. Let us now see what happens if some force is applied to the entity from the outside.

Suppose the natural, unperturbed cycle of the entity is given by the undulating line *AB,* which has an upward trend. Suppose further that some external force is applied at point *E* to reduce the depth of the downswing. Since every entity has its own internal momentum, its energy has to find an outlet in some other way. As a result, when the downswing is restrained from *V* to, say, *D,* the subsequent peak will be higher than the case would be otherwise. In other words, the effect of the external force will be to raise the peak at point *F* to somewhere above it, to, say, point *G*. The extent of the shift of *F* to *G* will be proportional to the preceding restraint over the downswing.

If the application of the external force is discontinued at some point, then the ensuing downswing will be deeper than the one preceding it. For instance, if the force were applied at *E* and not at the point of subsequent downturn, then the trough of the cycle would be at, say, *S* instead of *R*. On the other hand, if the force were applied continuously at each downturn, then the downswings would be brief and/or shallow, but the upswings would be at progressively higher peaks.

The result is that the external force would convert the natural cycle *AEVFRKB* into a controlled cycle such as *AEDGSTW*. The cyclical pattern cannot be eliminated; it can only be transformed, simply because the inner momentum or energy of an entity has to vent itself in some way. In the interest of enduring stability, essentially a new system has to be created out of the old, because each entity has its own momentum that generates a certain type of cycle. If the natural cycle is unstable, no external force can stabilize it for long; only a change in the natural rhythm of a system can generate lasting stability, and that means essentially creating a new entity with a relatively stable natural cycle of its own.

Let us now compare the time path illustrated in Chart 10 to the historical behavior of the rate of inflation, which had a natural cycle in the eighteenth and nineteenth centuries, when government intervention in the economy was minimal. In the upswing of the business cycle, the inflation rate would be positive; in the downswing, negative. When the Fed was established in 1914, the government began controlling the supply of money in order to eliminate or at least reduce the depth of the downswing. For a while this experiment was successful and the government was able to control downturns in the 1910s. But the inflation that occurred in the 1910s was higher than in any preceding decade in history. In other words, since the negative rate of inflation had been restrained by the creation of the Fed, the positive inflation rate turned out to be higher than that of any previous decade. Since the natural cycle of inflation, basically unstable, was not allowed to fully vent its energy in a business downturn, its expression had to be greater during the business upturn—a fact also substantiated by the economy's behavior since the Second World War. The cycle of inflation (as is clear from Chart 5 on page 94) reached its highest peak during the 1970s.

When another downturn came in 1929, the Fed did not take any action to control the money supply as it had in the 1910s; it simply failed to take any action whatsoever. Hence the business downswing and the resultant negative inflation were the deepest in history, culminating in the Great Depression of the 1930s. Now the government believed it had learned its lesson; the New Deal introduced extensive reforms curbing excessive banking and business practices. The government also acquired the counter-cyclical policy tools recommended by Keynes.

Unlike its "hands off" attitude in 1929, there has been no letup in government manipulation of and interference with the economy since the 1930s. Hence the business downswings and negative inflation rates have been restrained time and again, but the energy of the inflation cycle has found greater expression in its upswing. Chart 5 clearly shows that the cycle of inflation has had progressively higher peaks in the twentieth century than in the nineteenth. The same holds true with the cycle of money growth. There again, the cycle has had wider fluctuations in the current century—especially after the Fed was established—than in the previous century.

This is the point that will help us differentiate between superficial and fundamental reforms. With superficial reforms, short-run fluctuations are curtailed but long-run fluctuations increase. Fundamental reforms cause a lasting diminution in business oscillations. Chart 11 illustrates this case, where the

Chart 11 / **Impact of Fundamental Reforms**

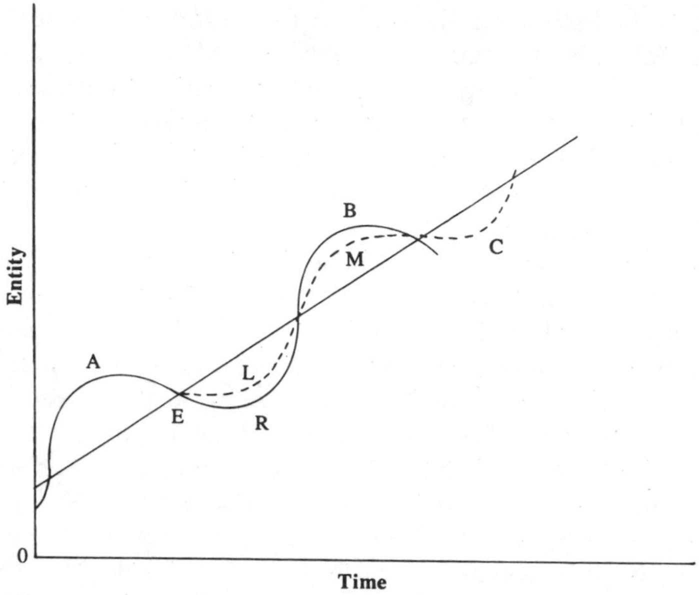

natural cycle of inflation *AERB* is transformed into a controlled cycle *AELMC*. Note that the cycle has not been eliminated; nor can it ever be, because straight-line evolution is not possible for any entity, no matter what. However, the amplitude of economic fluctuations can be reduced for a very long time with the aid of fundamental reforms. What happens then to the inner energy or dynamics of the economy? How will it find full expression? The answer is that we will essentially be creating a new and healthier entity. Since everything has its own rhythmical movement, the reforms have to be such that a *new* free-market economy, with a relatively stable natural cycle of its own, is created out of the current chaotic system.

Are such reforms possible? The reader has a right to be skeptical. If Keynesian economics, Monetarism, classical and neoclassical prescriptions, and every other economic theory have failed to produce long-run economic stability, is it ever possible to achieve it? Maybe such a formula just does not exist, because the best brains among the experts have not been able to discover it.

The problem is not with lack of brains, but with lack of motivation. Keynesians hold that capitalism is basically unstable but that the government can stabilize the system; Monetarists argue that the system is basically stable and that government intervention causes instability. What must be understood is that capitalism is fundamentally unstable, and the government's superficial interventions, while stabilizing it in the short run, compound its instability in the long run, when the fluctuations increase in amplitude.

We saw in Chapter 6 that depressions are caused primarily by extreme disparities in the distribution of wealth. In the age of acquisitors, it is the affluent class, the prime source of this inequity, that dominates society and determines who gets what. The instability of capitalism springs from this disparity in wealth. If it is reduced, the inherent energy of the system can be controlled and harnessed for the good of society.

Policies advocated by Keynesians, Monetarists, and others strike only at the symptoms of economic ills, not at their cause, the concentration of wealth. These policies, rather than stabilize the economy, add to its problems in the long run. But the time has come when superficial measures such as monetary and fiscal expansion will not work even in the short run.

Immediate Measures

The American economy displays two disturbing trends. One is, of course, the rising concentration of wealth and income, and the other is the mammoth budget deficit. Both have been created by the misguided tax cuts of 1981; neither shows signs of subsiding.

An obvious way to reverse these trends would be to restore the tax rates prevailing before President Reagan came to office. However, this would only partially solve the problem of the budget deficit and hardly create a dent in the enormous disparity of wealth. A study by the Joint Economic Committee of Congress indicates that in 1983 the top 1 percent of the U.S. population owned more than a third of the total wealth (see Table 1, page 118). Ever since the Second World War, the government has followed tax policies designed to reduce income and wealth inequalities, but with little success. The inheritance tax, progressive income tax, gift tax, etc., were riddled with so many loopholes that the rich were able to avoid paying their full share of taxes. In fact, the Tax Reform Act of 1986 leaves totally untouched the biggest factor in wealth inequality—the inheritance tax, which continues to favor the consolidation of wealth in the hands of a few.

Apart from removing all the loopholes, what the country needs is a *federal property tax* on that 1 percent of the population owning over a third of the wealth. Property taxes are currently levied by states and cities but not by the federal government. There is compelling need for such a federal tax today.

Much of the budget deficit is caused by high defense spending. The purpose of a strong defense presumably is to protect a person's life, liberty, and property from foreign enemies. Stated differently, an individual derives three main benefits from the maintenance of armed forces. A time-honored principle of taxation is that one should pay taxes in proportion to the benefits one receives. Since life and liberty are equally dear to everybody, but people differ in terms of the ownership of wealth, the wealthy ought to bear at least one-third of the total defense burden. Stated another way, since defense spending provides three major benefits—namely, the protection of life, liberty, and property—one-third of this expenditure should be borne by the owners of property.

Similar logic can be applied to all federal spending for the prevention of crime, because in this instance the benefits are much the same. In other words, one-third of federal expenditures for defense and the fight against crime should be borne by a federal property tax.

Certain types of property should be exempted from this tax. The necessities of daily life would fall into this category. Thus personal residence, car, clothing, furniture, etc., would be exempt. However, stocks, bonds, savings accounts, commercial real estate, and the like ought to be taxed at progressive rates. And the rates should be set so that the revenue from the tax equals one-third of the federal spending for defense and crime control.

By the end of 1987, federal spending for defense and law enforcement is expected to be around $400 billion. This means that about $133 billion should be collected from the federal property tax. This action alone would trim more than 60 percent of the budget deficit.

Benefits of the federal property tax would be considerable. Not only would it soften the problem of the budget deficit, it would also reverse the rising tide of wealth disparity. The solution of these problems would in turn head off the great depression of 1990 and buy us time to devise and implement remedies for a lasting cure.

What are the chances of the government's actually imposing such a tax before 1990? Slim to nonexistent! First, the government is dominated by the forces and lobbies of the affluent, and they are unlikely to support this tax even if the prevention of a depression is as much in their interest as that of the nation. Second, Congress is in no mood to get involved in yet another tax bill after spending more than two years hammering out the Tax Reform Act of 1986. There is simply not enough time between now and 1990 to enact such potentially divisive legislation involving a national property tax.

Does this mean that it is all over? No. There is no need ever to give up. The government can take other measures to at least soften the impact of the impending crisis. For example, we need to cool the euphoria that is currently intoxicating the financial markets. For if you don't want a hangover the next day, you should not get drunk the night before.

One step the government should take immediately to damp down the euphoria is to pass legislation restraining the banks and other financial institutions from lending money for business takeovers. The 1980s, like the 1920s, have been hit by a giant wave of mergers. I have nothing against mergers, so long as one business takes over another with the help of its own cash. But once the banks get involved, the financial system becomes even more fragile than before. In most cases, a merger fuels the fires of stock speculation and adds to the company debt. Share prices of the business being overtaken suddenly skyrocket, and banks end up financing this upsurge. Moreover, a company attempting to combat a bank-supported hostile takeover can greatly deplete its resources and damage its financial strength.

What is the end result? Debt of the merged companies has soared, and the wealth disparity has worsened as the stockholders become even richer than before. Keep in mind that the top 1 percent of wealth holders own as much as 50 percent of common stock in America.

Every depression has been preceded by a speculative bubble in asset markets. But if there is no bubble, there can be no bursting, and hence no depression. Banks must be restrained from fueling the speculative mania, which is now ominously building up. In other words, banks should not be allowed to lend money for business mergers.

Another step the government can take to cool the speculative fever is to increase margin requirements, currently varying from 3 percent to 5 percent, in commodity and futures markets. The requirement should be set at 50 percent of the purchase price, as is now the case in the stock market. In fact, I would urge the government to set up a commission of experts to investigate the whole question of speculative mania now in progress and offer suggestions as to how to calm it down.

Fundamental Economic Reforms

The federal property tax, restraints over banks, and increased margin requirements in commodity and futures markets would only buy us time without providing a long-term solution. For a lasting cure, we need to introduce fundamental reforms that eradicate economic as well as social ills. These reforms would create a new society with an ideal economy, which, in my view, should have the following features:

1. Its minimum wage rate satisfies a family's basic needs of food, shelter, clothing, education, and medical care.
2. It provides full incentive to everyone to work hard and enjoy the fruits of his physical and intellectual labor.
3. Its inflation and unemployment rates are low, but the growth rate is high.
4. It is subject to minimal disruptions from external forces, so that no one suffers undue hardships from unforeseen shocks that periodically afflict a society.
5. Its tax system is fair and free from loopholes.

These are features of a model economy where socioeconomic tensions are likely to be minimal. What kind of society can achieve this ideal?

It is clear from the outset that an essentially totalitarian system such as the Soviet government could never attain this ideal economy, because it could never permit its citizens free choice and incentives and still retain its absolutist character. Only a free-market society is capable of reaching this goal, provided government interference is minimal. For big government draws an excessive amount of resources away from the productive private sector and leads to bureaucratic waste and inefficiency. All that the government should do is protect the interests of the disadvantaged. The economic system should be such that it functions smoothly with minimum help from the state. The desirable attributes of the economy should be built into the system rather than be continually imposed from outside.

Adam Smith demonstrated as far back as 1776 that a free-market economy enjoys maximum efficiency and high growth. However, Smith's free enterprise system is characterized by keen competition among businessmen. Such competition tends to ensure that wealth and income disparities among individuals do not become too great; otherwise the extremely wealthy will be able to buy smaller firms and create monopolies, oligopolies, and other forms of uncompetitive markets. Lack of competition and concentration of wealth have moved together in history.

The history of Western nations, which come closest to meeting Adam Smith's assumptions, reveals that in the long run the relatively free-market economies indeed enjoy a high degree of efficiency, growth, and prosperity. However, such economies have also been convulsed time and again. This inherent tendency of Western nations can be eradicated only by minimizing wealth disparities and by creating a system where egalitarianism becomes part and parcel of the economy. The government cannot be called upon periodically to aid a crumbling structure, for in the end big government only makes matters worse. We need a system where the clamor for government intervention is the least, where unemployment compensation, food stamps, Medicaid, and other welfare programs are not needed. It is beyond the purpose and scope of this book to lay out the blueprint for an ideal system. Such a system has already been envisioned by P. R. Sarkar, the expounder of the law of social cycles, who calls it Prout, which is an acronym for Progressive (Pro), Utilization (u), Theory (t). Elsewhere I have discussed the merits and features of this system in detail.[31] Here I will merely sketch the basic outline of the Prout-based reforms which would give rise to a free enterprise society that possesses the attributes of such an ideal economy. These are admittedly far-reaching and profound changes, and if nothing else, they will serve to jolt us out of the unexamined assumptions of conventional economic wisdom.

1. Until the Proutist system is established, there should be a link between the minimum wage and the maximum wage. Specifically, the maximum salary in any industry should be no more than ten times the minimum wage.
2. Industries producing essential products and raw materials, such as oil, coal, and steel, should be divided into smaller competing units, so that monopolistic private producers cannot blackmail the entire society by withholding supplies.[32]
3. The majority stock of large corporations should be distributed among blue- and white-collar employees, whose elected representatives should constitute the board of directors.
4. Private initiative and investment should be limited to small corporations or proprietorships.
5. There should be ceilings on inherited wealth linked to the minimum wage.
6. The government budget should be balanced over the business cycle, that is, the budget should have a surplus when the economy is booming and a deficit when the economy is in a recession.

7. Money growth should equal the average growth of the economy over the business cycle. It should be raised during recessions and reduced during booms.
8. Except for essential industries such as those mentioned in item 2, government intervention in the economy should be minimum. It should aim mainly at maintaining competition among economic agents and promoting the interests of the disadvantaged.

These are the fundamental economic reforms that would eventually create the ideal economy described above. Notable features of this economy would be a government small in size and low inequality of wealth among social classes. There would be mass capitalism or industrial democracy in which representatives of blue- and white-collar employees would manage industries. Company profits, the main source of wealth inequality today, would be distributed among the masses, and wealth disparities, once minimized through inheritance taxes, would be held in check. In times of a recession, no employee would be laid off, as all employees would collectively manage the factories; only working hours would be reduced, so that all would equally share the burden of a business contraction. There would then be no need for unemployment compensation and the resultant bureaucracy.

Similarly, during a boom all would share the fruits of prosperity. With low wealth disparities, there would be no speculative manias and hence no great depressions. In short, with the aid of fundamental economic reforms, we would not only avoid cataclysmic depressions but would also create an ideal economy equitable to all. This would be an economy of high productivity and growth, because workers, with ownership, pride, and a stake in the company's future, would have a special incentive to work hard.

Keynesian economics, Monetarism, and other theories have not been able to exorcise Western society of the curse of depressions, because the reforms they advocate strike only at the symptoms of the age-old disease. However, Prout-based reforms would eliminate the cause of the malady and basically create a new free-market system, which would have a new natural and relatively stable rhythm of its own.

I hope, of course, that the government will not ignore this advice. Even if it accepts only some of these suggestions, the depression can be prevented or blunted. If not, we will certainly find ourselves in the worst economic turmoil in history—in the Great Depression of 1990. And as that time approaches, only those of us who have taken the defensive measures I have suggested in Chapter 8 will manage to survive.

APPENDIX

To Chapter 3

The data underlying Chart 1 have been obtained from the following sources: Milton Friedman and Anna Schwartz, *A Monetary History of the United States, 1867–1960*, Princeton University Press, 1983; John Gurley and Edward Shaw, "The Growth of Debt and Money in the United States," *Review of Economics and Statistics*, August 1957, p. 258; Ravi Batra, "The Long-Run Cycles of Money Growth and Inflation in the United States," *Renaissance Universal Journal*, Vol. 2–3, Fall 1984.

These data are presented in the following table, which is taken directly from Batra's article. The table also contains figures for wholesale prices and inflation rates per decade, and these figures form the basis of Charts 2 and 3 in Chapter 4.

The Great Depression of 1990

Decennial Average Wholesale Price Index 1910-14 = 100, Old M2, Inflation Rates, and Money Growth Rates

Decades	AP	M2 (in billions of dollars)*	Inflation Rate (%)	Money Growth (%)
1740–1750	68	—	—	—
1750–1760	68	—	0	—
1760–1770	77	.004	13.2	—
1770–1780	116	.010	50.6	150.0
1780–1790	128	.0196	10.3	96.0
1790–1800	114	.030	−10.9	53.1
1800–1810	129	.067	13.2	123.3
1810–1820	144	.084	11.6	25.4
1820–1830	100	.126	−30.6	50.0
1830–1840	101	.232	1.0	84.1
1840–1850	84	.344	−16.8	48.3
1850–1860	97	.605	15.5	75.8
1860–1870	143	1.39	47.4	129.7
1870–1880	116	2.28	−18.9	64.0
1880–1890	91	3.99	−21.6	75.0
1890–1900	75	6.94	−17.4	73.9
1900–1910	90	13.61	20.0	96.1
1910–1920	138	34.76	53.3	155.4
1920–1930	149	45.16	8.0	29.9
1930–1940	112	57.89	−24.8	28.2
1940–1950	175	152.50	56.3	163.4
1950–1960	255	213.10	45.7	39.7
1960–1970	281	420.20	10.2	97.2
1970–1980	463	1135.10	64.8	170.1

* Each M2 is for the end of the decade. Thus .004 is M2 for 1770, and so on. Using the 1770s as an example, money-growth rates are obtained by the formula:

$$\frac{\text{M2 in 1780} - \text{M2 in 1770}}{\text{M2 in 1770}} \times 100 = \frac{.010 - .004}{.004} \times 100 = 150$$

AP = average WPI in decade.

APPENDIX

To Chapter 4

The WPI data contained in the following table have been obtained as follows: for 1749–1970, *Historical Statistics of the United States*, Washington, D.C., 1976 (series 52, pp. 201–202, and series 23, p. 199); for 1970–85, *Economic Report of the President*, Washington, D.C., 1986. See also Ravi Batra, *Renaissance Universal Journal*, Vol. 2–3, Fall 1984.

In series 52, three observations are missing for the years 1782–84. This was the period immediately following the American Revolution and prices were rapidly falling. The three missing observations were obtained by assuming that in each of these years prices fell at the same rate.

Similarly, figures were missing for 1788 and 1792, and since no trends are clear at these times, figures from the prior year were repeated for these years. For the decennial average wholesale price index and inflation rates, which are based on the following table, see the table in the Appendix to Chapter 3.

Wholesale Price Index (WPI) 1749–1985
1910–14 = 100

Year	WPI	Year	WPI	Year	WPI	Year	WPI	Year	WPI
1749	68	1771	79	1793	102	1815	170	1837	115
1750	60	1772	89	1794	108	1816	151	1838	110
1751	65	1773	84	1795	131	1817	151	1839	112
1752	66	1774	76	1796	146	1818	147	1840	95
1753	65	1775	75	1797	131	1819	125	1841	92
1754	65	1776	86	1798	122	1820	106	1842	82
1755	66	1777	123	1799	126	1821	102	1843	75
1756	66	1778	140	1800	129	1822	106	1844	77
1757	65	1779	226	1801	142	1823	103	1845	83
1758	70	1780	225	1802	117	1824	98	1846	83
1759	79	1781	216	1803	118	1825	103	1847	90
1760	79	1782	175	1804	126	1826	99	1848	82
1761	77	1783	142	1805	141	1827	98	1849	82
1762	87	1784	115	1806	134	1828	97	1850	84
1763	79	1785	92	1807	130	1829	96	1851	83
1764	74	1786	90	1808	115	1830	91	1852	88
1765	72	1787	90	1809	130	1831	94	1853	97
1766	73	1788	90	1810	131	1832	95	1854	108
1767	77	1789	86	1811	126	1833	95	1855	110
1768	74	1790	90	1812	131	1834	90	1856	105
1769	77	1791	85	1813	162	1835	100	1857	111
1770	77	1792	85	1814	182	1836	114	1858	93

Year	WPI	Year	WPI	Year	WPI	Year	WPI	Year	WPI
1859	95	1885	85	1911	95	1937	126	1963	268
1860	93	1886	82	1912	101	1938	115	1964	268
1861	89	1887	85	1913	102	1939	113	1965	274
1862	104	1888	86	1914	100	1940	115	1966	283
1863	133	1889	81	1915	101	1941	128	1967	283
1864	193	1890	82	1916	125	1942	144	1968	290
1865	185	1891	82	1917	172	1943	151	1969	302
1866	174	1892	76	1918	192	1944	152	1970	313
1867	162	1893	78	1919	202	1945	155	1971	323
1868	158	1894	70	1920	225	1946	176	1972	333
1869	151	1895	71	1921	142	1947	217	1973	363
1870	135	1896	68	1922	141	1948	235	1974	419
1871	130	1897	68	1923	147	1949	223	1975	464
1872	136	1898	71	1924	143	1950	232	1976	485
1873	133	1899	76	1925	151	1951	258	1977	516
1874	126	1900	82	1926	146	1952	251	1978	556
1875	118	1901	81	1927	140	1953	248	1979	618
1876	110	1902	86	1928	142	1954	248	1980	702
1877	106	1903	87	1929	139	1955	249	1981	766
1878	91	1904	88	1930	126	1956	257	1982	797
1879	90	1905	88	1931	107	1957	264	1983	810
1880	100	1906	91	1932	95	1958	268	1984	824
1881	103	1907	95	1933	96	1959	269	1985	831
1882	108	1908	92	1934	109	1960	269		
1883	101	1909	99	1935	117	1961	268		
1884	93	1910	103	1936	118	1962	269		

APPENDIX

To Chapter 5

The data underlying Chart 6 are presented in Appendix Tables 1 and 2, which in turn are obtained from the following sources. These two tables lead to Appendix Table 3, which underlies the cycles graphed in Chart 6.

1. Ronald Penoyer, *Directory of Regulatory Agencies*, Center for the Study of American Business, Washington University, St. Louis, 1981 and 1982.
2. Bureau of the Budget, *United States at War*, Washington, D.C., 1947.
3. William F. Willoughby, *Government Organization in War Time and After*, Macmillan, London, 1919.
4. Gilbert Fite and Jim Reese, *An Economic History of the United States*, Houghton Mifflin, Boston, 1973.
5. Martin Primack and James Willis, *An Economic History of the United States*, Benjamin Cummings, Menlo Park, Calif., 1980.
6. Martin Schnitzer, *Contemporary Government Relations*, Houghton Mifflin, Boston, 1983.

APPENDIX

Table 1

Chronology of Major Regulatory Bodies

1830–1840
Patent and Trademark Office, 1836

1840–1850
None

1850–1860
None

1860–1870
1. Comptroller of the Currency, 1863
2. Copyright Office, 1870

1870–1880
Copyright Office, 1870

1880–1890
Interstate Commerce Commission, 1887

1890–1900

Army Corps of Engineers, 1899

1900–1910

Antitrust Division, 1903

1910–1920

1. Federal Reserve System (Board of Governors), 1913
2. Federal Trade Commission, 1914
3. Coast Guard, 1915
4. Tariff Commission, 1916
5. Federal Power Commission, 1920

In addition to these agencies, the following regulatory bodies were set up during the 1910s for the successful prosecution of the First World War, which began in 1914.

6. Council of National Defense, 1916
7. Shipping Board, 1916
8. Food Administration, 1917
9. Fuel Administration, 1917
10. Railroad Administration, 1917
11. War Industries Board, 1917
12. War Trade Board, 1917
13. War Finance Corporation, 1918
14. Labor Administration, 1918

1920–1930

1. Federal Power Commission, 1920
2. Commodity Exchange Authority, 1922
3. Bureau of Customs, 1927

1930–1940

1. Food and Drug Administration, 1931
2. Federal Home Loan Bank Board, 1932
3. Farm Credit Administration, 1933
4. Federal Deposit Insurance Corporation, 1933
5. Federal Communications Commission, 1934
6. Securities and Exchange Commission, 1934
7. National Labor Relations Board, 1935
8. Maritime Administration, 1936
9. Agricultural Marketing Service and Other Agencies, 1937
10. Civil Aeronautics Authority, 1938
11. Fish and Wildlife Service, 1940

1940–1950

1. Fish and Wildlife Service, 1940
2. Atomic Energy Commission, 1946

In addition to these agencies, the following regulatory bodies were established during the 1940s for the successful prosecution of the Second World War.

3. Board of Economic Warfare
4. Food Distribution Administration
5. Food Production Administration
6. Foreign Economic Administration
7. National Defense Advisory Commission
8. National Housing Agency
9. National Wage Stabilization Board
10. National War Labor Board
11. Office for Emergency Management
12. Office of Economic Stabilization
13. Office of Economic Warfare
14. Office of Export Control
15. Office of Petroleum Coordinator for National Defense
16. Office of Price Administration
17. Office of Production Management
18. Retraining and Reemployment Administration
19. Surplus Property Administration
20. Wage Adjustment Board for the Construction Industry
21. War Insurance Corporation
22. War Manpower Commission
23. War Production Board
24. War Shipping Administration

1950–1960

1. Renegotiation Board, 1951
2. Foreign Agricultural Service, 1953
3. Small Business Administration, 1953
4. Federal Aviation Agency, 1958

1960–1970

1. Agricultural Stabilization and Conservation Service, 1961
2. Labor-Management Services Administration, 1963
3. Equal Employment Opportunity Commission, 1964

4. Federal Highway Administration, 1966
5. National Transportation Safety Board, 1966
6. Federal Railroad Administration, 1966
7. Council on Environmental Quality, 1969
8. Cost Accounting Standards Board, 1970
9. Environmental Protection Agency, 1970
10. National Credit Union Administration, 1970
11. National Highway Traffic Safety Administration, 1970
12. Occupational Safety and Health Administration, 1970

1970–1980

1. Cost Accounting Standards Board, 1970
2. Environmental Protection Agency, 1970
3. National Credit Union Administration, 1970
4. National Highway Traffic Safety Administration, 1970
5. Occupational Safety and Health Administration, 1970
6. Employment Standards Administration, 1971
7. Occupational Safety and Health Review Commission, 1971
8. Bureau of Alcohol, Tobacco, and Firearms, 1972
9. Consumer Product Safety Commission, 1972
10. Domestic and International Business Administration, 1972
11. Drug Enforcement Administration, 1973
12. Federal Energy Administration, 1973
13. Mining Enforcement and Safety Administration, 1973
14. Council on Wage and Price Stability, 1974
15. Federal Election Commission, 1975
16. Materials Transportation Bureau, 1975
17. Federal Grain Inspection Service, 1976
18. Office of Neighborhoods, Voluntary Associations, and Consumer Protection, 1977
19. Office of Surface Mining Reclamation and Enforcement, 1977
20. Office of the Federal Inspector of the Alaska Natural Gas Transportation System, 1979

1980–1984

1. Packers and Stockyards Administration, Department of Agriculture, 1982

APPENDIX

Table 2

Regulatory Legislation per Decade

1760–1770

1. Sugar Act, 1764
2. Prohibition against printing paper money, 1764
3. Stamp Act, 1765
4. Townsend Revenue Act, 1767

1770–1780

1. Tea Act, 1773
2. Coercive or Intolerable Acts, 1774
3. Bill to appoint a Treasurer, 1775
4. Funding Act, 1775
5. Bill to strengthen the Treasury, 1776
6. Funding Act, 1776
7. Bill to open American ports to all nations except England, 1776
8. Bill to establish an Office of Accounts, 1776
9. Funding Act, 1777
10. Bill to appoint Loan Commissioners, 1777
11. Bill to appoint Boards of Treasury, 1778

12. Funding Act, 1778
13. Bill to have a commercial agreement with France, 1778
14. Bill to strengthen the Boards of Treasury, 1779
15. Funding Act, 1779
16. Law regarding specie value of currency, 1780

1780–1790

1. Law regarding specie value of currency, 1780
2. Law regarding specie value of currency, 1781
3. Bank of North America Act, 1781
4. Law establishing the Office of Superintendent of Finance, 1781
5. Land Ordinance, 1784
6. Land Ordinance, 1785
7. Land Ordinance, 1786
8. Funding Act, 1790

1790–1800

1. Funding Act, 1790
2. Whiskey Tax Act, 1791
3. First United States Bank Act, 1791
4. Tariff Act, 1792
5. Revenue Act, 1794
6. Land Act, 1796
7. Land Act, 1800

1800–1810

1. Land Act, 1800
2. Revenue Act, 1802
3. Tariff Act, 1804
4. Land Act, 1804
5. National Turnpike Act, 1806
6. Debt Conversion Act, 1807
7. Slave Importation Law, 1807
8. Tariff Act, 1807
9. Embargo Act, 1807
10. Non-intercourse Act, 1809

1810–1820

1. Tariff Act, 1812
2. Revenue Act, 1813
3. Second United States Bank Act, 1816
4. Tariff Act, 1816
5. Tariff Act, 1818

6. Land Act, 1819
7. Land Act, 1820

1820–1830

1. Land Act, 1820
2. Pension Act, 1823
3. Tariff Act, 1824
4. Tariff Act, 1828
5. Preemption Act, 1830
6. Tariff Act, 1830

1830–1840

1. Preemption Act, 1830
2. Tariff Act, 1830
3. Tariff Act, 1832
4. Tariff Act, 1833
5. Coinage Act, 1834
6. Deposit Act, 1836
7. Patent Act, 1836
8. Act requiring federal inspection of steamboats, 1836
9. Independent Treasury Bill, 1840

1840–1850

1. Independent Treasury Bill, 1840
2. Preemption Act, 1841
3. Tariff Act, 1842
4. Independent Treasury Bill, 1846
5. Tariff Act, 1846

1850–1860

1. Coinage Act, 1853
2. Kansas–Nebraska Act, 1854
3. Graduation Act, 1854
4. Tariff Act, 1857
5. Independent Treasury Act, 1857

1860–1870

1. Morrill Tariff Act, 1861
2. Loan Act, 1861
3. Tax Act, 1861
4. Morrill Land Grant Act, 1862
5. Revenue Act, 1862
6. Homestead Act, 1862

7. Tariff Act, 1862
8. Pacific Railway Act, 1862
9. Tariff Act, 1863
10. National Bank Act, 1864
11. Currency Act, 1863
12. Revenue Act, 1863
13. National Bank Act, 1864
14. Revenue Act, 1864
15. Revenue Act, 1865
16. Funding Act, 1866
17. Refunding Act, 1870
18. Copyright Act, 1870

1870–1880

1. Refunding Act, 1870
2. Copyright Act, 1870
3. Tariff Act, 1873
4. Coinage Act, 1873
5. Timber Culture Act, 1873
6. Tariff Act, 1875
7. Desert-Land Act, 1877
8. Timber and Stone Act, 1878
9. Bland–Allison Act, 1878
10. Pension–Arrears Act, 1879

1880–1890

1. Immigration Act, 1882
2. Tariff Act, 1883
3. Hatch Act, 1883
4. Law regarding animal and plant health inspection, 1884
5. Interstate Commerce Act, 1887
6. Sherman Silver Purchase Act, 1890
7. Sherman Anti-Trust Act, 1890
8. McKinley Tariff Act, 1890
9. Morrill Act, 1890
10. Law regarding importation of certain animals, 1890

1890–1900

1. Sherman Silver Purchase Act, 1890
2. Sherman Anti-Trust Act, 1890
3. McKinley Tariff Act, 1890
4. Morrill Act, 1890
5. Law regarding importation of certain animals, 1890

6. Forest Reserve Act, 1891
7. Wilson–Gorman Act, 1894
8. Dockery Act, 1894
9. Dingley Tariff, 1897
10. Tea Importation Act, 1897
11. River and Harbor Act, 1899
12. Currency Act, 1900
13. Gold Standard Act, 1900
14. Lacey Act, 1900

1900–1910

1. Currency Act, 1900
2. Gold Standard Act, 1900
3. Lacey Act, 1900
4. Law regarding animal and plant health inspection, 1903
5. Elkins Act, 1903
6. Expediting Act, 1903
7. Law regarding animal and plant health inspection, 1905
8. Law regarding dredged material dumping, 1905
9. Pure Food and Drug Act, 1906
10. Hepburn Act, 1906
11. Copyright Act, 1909
12. Payne–Aldrich Act, 1909
13. Mine Safety Act, 1910
14. Mann–Elkins Act, 1910

1910–1920

1. Mine Safety Act, 1910
2. Mann–Elkins Act, 1910
3. Plant Quarantine Act, 1912
4. Panama Canal Act, 1912
5. Income-Tax Act, 1913
6. Underwood Tariff Act, 1913
7. Federal Reserve Act, 1913
8. Clayton Act, 1914
9. Federal Trade Commission Act, 1914
10. Coast Guard Act, 1915
11. Adamson Act, 1916
12. Shipping Act, 1916
13. Highway Act, 1916
14. National Defense Act, 1916
15. U.S. Warehouse Act, 1916

16. Federal Employee Compensation Act, 1916
17. Federal Farm Loan Act, 1916
18. Esch Car Service Act, 1917
19. Liberty Loan Act, 1917
20. Lever Food and Fuel Control Act, 1917
21. Law regarding danger zones in navigable waters, 1918
22. Pittman Act, 1918
23. Migratory Bird Treaty Act, 1918
24. Jones Act, 1920
25. Esch–Cummins Transportation Act, 1920
26. Water Power Act, 1920
27. Mineral Lands Leasing Act, 1920
28. Merchant Marine Act, 1920

In addition to the above laws, the following regulatory acts relate to the successful prosecution of the war effort during the 1910s:

29. Council of National Defense, 1916
30. National Research Council, 1918
31. Board of Inventions, 1917
32. Trading with the Enemy Act, 1917
33. War Finance Corporation Act, 1918
34. Committee on Coal Production, 1917
35. Agricultural Production Stimulation Act, 1917
36. Fuel Production Act, 1917
37. Aircraft Board, 1917
38. American Relief Administration, 1919
39. Board of Control of Labor Standards in Army Clothing, 1917
40. Board of Mediation and Conciliation, 1913
41. Board of Railway Wages and Working Conditions, 1918
42. Bureau of Industrial Housing and Transportation, 1918
43. Bureau of War Risk Insurance, 1914
44. Commercial Economy Board, 1917
45. Emergency Fleet Corporation, 1917
46. Food Administration, 1917
47. National Research Council, 1918
48. Labor Administration, 1918
49. Munitions Standards Board, 1917
50. National Adjustment Commission, 1917
51. Railroad Administration, 1917
52. Shipping Board, 1916

53. Sugar Equalization Board, 1918
54. War Credits Board, 1917
55. War Industries Board, 1917
56. War Labor Policies Board, 1918
57. War Trade Board, 1917

1920–1930

1. Jones Act, 1920
2. Esch–Cummins Transportation Act, 1920
3. Water Power Act, 1920
4. Mineral Lands Leasing Act, 1920
5. Merchant Marine Act, 1920
6. Emergency Tariff Act, 1921
7. Revenue Act, 1921
8. Anti-Trust Exemption Law, 1921
9. Anti-Dumping Act, 1921
10. Packers and Stockyards Act, 1921
11. Immigration Act, 1921
12. Budget and Accounting Act, 1921
13. Fordney–McCumber Act, 1922
14. Commodity Exchange Act, 1922
15. Filled Milk Act, 1923
16. Intermediate Credits Act, 1923
17. Revenue Act, 1924
18. Capper–Volstead Act, 1926
19. Black Bass Act, 1926
20. Revenue Act, 1926
21. Railroad Labor Act, 1926
22. Produce Act, 1927
23. Customs Bureau Act, 1927
24. Longshoremen's and Harbor Workers' Compensation Act, 1927
25. McFaden Branch Banking Act, 1927
26. Jones–White Act, 1928
27. Revenue Act, 1928
28. Migratory Bird Act, 1929
29. Agricultural Marketing Act, 1929
30. Smoot–Hawley Tariff Act, 1930
31. Perishable Agricultural Act, 1930

1930–1940

1. Smoot–Hawley Tariff Act, 1930
2. Perishable Agricultural Act, 1930

3. Agricultural Appropriations Act, 1931
4. Animal Damage Control Act, 1931
5. Davis–Bacon Act, 1931
6. Federal Home Loan Bank Act, 1932
7. Federal Reserve Act, 1933
8. Home Owners Loan Act, 1933
9. Securities Act, 1933
10. Banking Act, 1933
11. Agriculture Adjustment Act, 1933
12. Intercoastal Shipping Act, 1933
13. Securities Exchange Act, 1934
14. Communications Act, 1934
15. Federal Credit Union Act, 1934
16. National Housing Act, 1934
17. Fish and Wildlife Coordination Act, 1934
18. Migratory Bird Hunting Stamp Act, 1934
19. Gold Reserve Act, 1934
20. Soil Conservation and Domestic Allotments Act, 1935
21. Anti-Smuggling Act, 1935
22. Tobacco Inspection Act, 1935
23. Federal Alcohol Administration Act, 1935
24. National Labor Relations Act, 1935
25. Federal Power Act, 1935
26. Banking Act, 1935
27. Motor Carrier Act, 1935
28. Public Utility Holding Company Act, 1935
29. Robinson–Patman Act, 1936
30. Public Contracts Act, 1936
31. Liquor Enforcement Act, 1936
32. Law Regarding North Atlantic Vessel Operators, 1936
33. Agricultural Marketing Agreement Act, 1937
34. Federal Aid in Wildlife Restoration Act, 1937
35. Bankruptcy Act, 1938
36. Civil Aeronautics Act, 1938
37. Natural Gas Act, 1938
38. Fair Labor Standard Act, 1938
39. Agricultural Adjustment Act, 1938
40. Food, Drug and Cosmetic Act, 1938
41. Federal Seed Act, 1939
42. Trust Indenture Act, 1939
43. Investment Company Act, 1940

44. Investment Advisers Act, 1940
45. Wool Products Labelling Act, 1940
46. Bald Eagle Protection Act, 1940
47. Reorganization Plan No. 3, 1940
48. Motorboat Act, 1940

1940–1950

1. Investment Company Act, 1940
2. Investment Advisers Act, 1940
3. Wool Products Labelling Act, 1940
4. Bald Eagle Protection Act, 1940
5. Reorganization Plan No. 3, 1940
6. Motorboat Act, 1940
7. Organic Act, 1944
8. Public Health Services Act, 1944
9. Administrative Procedure Act, 1946
10. Agricultural Marketing Act, 1946
11. Atomic Energy Act, 1946
12. Lanham Trademark Act, 1946
13. Law Regarding Animal and Plant Health Inspection, 1947
14. Labor-Management Relations Act, 1947
15. Explosives and Dangerous Articles Act, 1948
16. Reed–Bullwinkle Act, 1948
17. Export Control Act, 1949
18. First Revenue Act, 1950
19. Celler–Kefauver Act, 1950
20. Defense Production Act, 1950
21. Federal Deposit Insurance Act, 1950
22. Federal Aid in Fish Restoration Act, 1950

In addition to the above regulatory laws, the following agencies were established during the 1940s by Executive Order to regulate the economy in wartime. These Executive Orders had the same force as economic legislation passed by Congress.

23. Advisory Board on Just Compensation
24. Board of Economic Warfare
25. Civilian Production Administration
26. Coal Mines Administrator
27. Colonial Mica Corporation
28. Combined Food Board

29. Combined Production and Resources Board
30. Combined Raw Materials Board
31. Combined Shipping Adjustment Board
32. Defense Plant Corporation
33. Defense Supplies Corporation
34. Food Distribution Administration
35. Food Production Administration
36. Foreign Economic Administration
37. Foreign Funds Control
38. National Defense Advisory Commission
39. National Defense Mediation Board
40. National Housing Agency
41. National Mediation Board
42. National Wage Stabilization Board
43. National War Labor Board
44. Office for Coordination of National Defense Purchases
45. Office for Emergency Management
46. Office of Agricultural Defense Relations
47. Office of Contract Settlement
48. Office of Defense Health and Welfare Service
49. Office of Defense Transportation
50. Office of Economic Stabilization
51. Office of Economic Warfare
52. Office of Export Control
53. Office of Fishery Coordination
54. Office of Merchant Ship Control
55. Office of Petroleum Coordinator for National Defense
56. Office of Price Administration
57. Office of Production Management
58. Office of Production Research and Development
59. Office of Scientific Research and Development
60. Petroleum Administration for War
61. Priorities Board
62. Reconstruction Finance Corporation
63. Retraining and Reemployment Administration
64. Rubber Development Corporation
65. Smaller War Plants Corporation
66. Southwestern Power Administration
67. Steel Recovery Corporation
68. Surplus Property Administration
69. U.S. Commercial Company
70. Wage Adjustment Board for the Construction Industry

71. War Assets Corporation
72. War Contracts Price Adjustment Board
73. War Food Administration
74. War Hemp Industries
75. War Insurance Corporation
76. War Manpower Commission
77. War Production Board
78. War Resources Board
79. War Shipping Administration
80. War Resources Council

1950–1960

1. Defense Production Act, 1950
2. Federal Deposit Insurance Corporation, 1950
3. Federal Aid in Fish Restoration Act, 1950
4. First Revenue Act, 1950
5. Second Revenue Act, 1950
6. Celler–Kefauver Act, 1950
7. Revenue Act, 1951
8. Taft–Humphrey Act, 1951
9. Renegotiation Act, 1951
10. Fur Products Labelling Act, 1951
11. Patent Act, 1952
12. McGuire Keogh Act, 1952
13. Small Business Act, 1953
14. Reorganization Plan No. 2, 1953
15. Outer Continental Shelf Lands Act, 1953
16. Agricultural Act, 1954
17. Atomic Energy Act, 1954
18. Flammable Fabrics Act, 1954
19. Internal Revenue Code, 1954
20. Housing Act, 1954
21. Anti-Trust Improvement Act, 1955
22. Federal Home Loan Act, 1955
23. Bank Holding Company Act, 1956
24. Fish and Wildlife Act, 1956
25. Fair-Labor Standards Act, 1956
26. Guidelines for Inspection of Passenger Vessels, 1956
27. Refrigerator Safety Act, 1956
28. Federal Plant Pests Act, 1957
29. Poultry Products Inspection Act, 1957
30. Federal Aviation Act, 1958

31. Teller Act, 1958
32. Humane Slaughter Act, 1958
33. Food Additives Amendment, 1958
34. Small Business Act, 1958
35. Small Business Investment Act, 1958
36. Textile Fiber Products Identification Act, 1958
37. Landrum–Griffin Act, 1959
38. Bank Merger Act, 1960
39. Great Lakes Pilotage Act, 1960
40. Hazardous Substances Act, 1960
41. Color Additives Amendments, 1960

1960–1970

1. Great Lakes Pilotage Act, 1960
2. Hazardous Substances Act, 1960
3. Color Additives Amendments, 1960
4. Bank Merger Act, 1960
5. Act of September 6, 1961
6. Oil Pollution Act, 1961
7. Wetlands Act, 1961
8. Act of July 2, 1962
9. Drug Amendments Act, 1962
10. Refuge Recreation Act, 1962
11. Bank Service Corporation Act, 1962
12. Communications Satellite Act, 1962
13. Trade Expansion Act, 1962
14. Equal Pay Act, 1963
15. Farm Labor Contractor Registration Act, 1963
16. Civil Rights Act, 1964
17. Meat Import Act, 1964
18. Highway Beautification Act, 1965
19. Executive Order, 1965
20. Service Contract Act, 1965
21. Anadromous Fish Conservation Act, 1965
22. Public Works and Economic Development Act, 1965
23. Federal Laboratory Animal Welfare Act, 1966
24. National Traffic and Motor Vehicle Safety Act, 1966
25. Highway Safety Act, 1966
26. Department of Transportation Act, 1966
27. Fair Packaging and Labelling Act, 1966
28. Federal Hazardous Substances Act, 1966

29. Federal Metal and Non-Metallic Mine Safety Act, 1966
30. Public Law 89-777, 1966
31. Department of Transportation Act, 1966
32. Clean Air Act, 1967
33. Federal Meat Inspection Act, 1967
34. Age Discrimination in Employment Act, 1967
35. Agricultural Fair Practices Act, 1968
36. Omnibus Crime Control and Safe Streets Act, 1968
37. Interstate Land Sales Full Disclosure Act, 1968
38. Radiation Control for Health and Safety Act, 1968
39. Gun Control Act, 1968
40. Consumer Credit Protection Act, 1968
41. Open Housing Act, 1968
42. Truth-in-Lending Act, 1968
43. Bank Protection Act, 1968
44. Public Law 90-298, 1968
45. Federal Coal Mine Health and Safety Act, 1969
46. Construction Safety Act, 1969
47. National Wildlife Refuge System Administration Act, 1969
48. National Environmental Policy Act, 1969
49. Natural Gas Pipeline Safety Act, 1969
50. Export Administration Act, 1969
51. Wheat Research and Promotion Act, 1970
52. Airport and Airway Revenue Act, 1970
53. Organized Crime Control Act, 1970
54. Rail Passenger Service Act, 1970
55. Federal Railroad Safety Act, 1970
56. Comprehensive Drug Abuse Prevention and Control Act, 1970
57. Horse Protection Act, 1970
58. Water Bank Act, 1970
59. Plant Variety Protection Act, 1970
60. Egg Products Inspection Act, 1970
61. Poison Prevention Packaging Act, 1970
62. Highway Safety Act, 1970
63. Occupational Safety and Health Act, 1970
64. National Environmental Improvement Act, 1970
65. Reorganization Plan No. 3, 1970
66. Reorganization Plan No. 4, 1970
67. Water Quality Improvement Act, 1970
68. National Credit Union Administration Act, 1970
69. Home Finance Act, 1970

70. National Credit Union Share Insurance Act, 1970
71. Bank Records and Foreign Transactions Act, 1970
72. Fair Credit Reporting Act, 1970
73. Disaster Relief Act, 1970

1970–1980

1. Wheat Research and Promotion Act, 1970
2. Airport and Airway Revenue Act, 1970
3. Organized Crime Control Act, 1970
4. Rail Passenger Service Act, 1970
5. Federal Railroad Safety Act, 1970
6. Comprehensive Drug Abuse Prevention and Control Act, 1970
7. Horse Protection Act, 1970
8. Water Bank Act, 1970
9. Plant Variety Protection Act, 1970
10. Egg Products Inspection Act, 1970
11. Poison Prevention Packaging Act, 1970
12. Highway Safety Act, 1970
13. Occupational Safety and Health Act, 1970
14. National Environmental Improvement Act, 1970
15. Reorganization Plan No. 3, 1970
16. Reorganization Plan No. 4, 1970
17. Water Quality Improvement Act, 1970
18. National Credit Union Administration Act, 1970
19. Home Finance Act, 1970
20. National Credit Union Share Insurance Act, 1970
21. Bank Records and Foreign Transactions Act, 1970
22. Fair Credit Reporting Act, 1970
23. Disaster Relief Act, 1970
24. Federal Boat Safety Act, 1971
25. Lead-Based Paint Poisoning Prevention Act, 1971
26. Postal Reorganization Act, 1971
27. Alaska Native Claims Settlement Act, 1971
28. Farm Credit Act, 1971
29. Ports and Waterways Safety Act, 1972
30. Federal Water Pollution Control Act Amendments, 1972
31. Motor Vehicle Information and Cost Saving Act, 1972
32. Consumer Product Safety Act, 1972
33. Equal Employment Opportunity Act, 1972
34. Federal Insecticide, Fungicide, and Rodenticide Act, 1972
35. Marine Mammal Protection Act, 1972

36. Noise Control Act, 1972
37. Coastal Zone Management Act, 1972
38. Marine Protection, Research, and Sanctuaries Act, 1972
39. Public Law 91-416, 1972
40. Reorganization Plan No. 2, 1973
41. Federal Aid Highway Act, 1973
42. Regional Rail Reorganization Act, 1973
43. Rehabilitation Act, 1973
44. Endangered Species Act, 1973
45. Emergency Petroleum Allocation Act, 1973
46. NOW Accounts Act, 1973
47. Trans-Alaska Pipeline Authorization Act, 1973
48. Consolidated Farm and Rural Development Act, 1973
49. Narcotic Addict Treatment Act, 1974
50. National Mobile Home Construction and Safety Standards Act, 1974
51. Real Estate Settlement Procedures Act, 1974
52. Trade Act, 1974
53. Deepwater Port Act, 1974
54. Independent Safety Board Act, 1974
55. Health Care Institutions Act, 1974
56. Employee Retirement Income Security Act, 1974
57. Vietnam Era Veterans Readjustment Assistance Act, 1974
58. Federal Energy Act, 1974
59. Federal Energy Administration Act, 1974
60. Energy Supply and Environmental Coordination Act, 1974
61. Energy Reorganization Act, 1974
62. Safe Drinking Water Act, 1974
63. Fair Credit Billing Act, 1974
64. Equal Credit Opportunity Act, 1974
65. Act of October 23, 1974
66. Trade Expansion Act, 1974
67. Council on Wage and Price Stability Act, 1974
68. Federal Election Campaign Act Amendments of 1974
69. Hazardous Material Transportation Act, 1975
70. Energy Policy and Conservation Act, 1975
71. Home Mortgage Disclosure Act, 1975
72. Magnuson-Moss Warranty Federal Trade Commission Improvement Act, 1975
73. Railroad Revitalization and Regulatory Reform Act, 1976
74. Medical Devices Amendments, 1976

75. International Security Assistance and Arms Control Act, 1976
76. Airport and Airway Development Act Amendments, 1976
77. Hart-Scott-Rodino Antitrust Improvement Act, 1976
78. Crime Control Act, 1976
79. U.S. Grain Standards Act, 1976
80. Energy Conservation and Production Act, 1976
81. Toxic Substances Control Act, 1976
82. Resource Conservation and Recovery Act, 1976
83. Consumer Leasing Act, 1976
84. Act of October 19, 1976
85. Food and Agriculture Act, 1977
86. Federal Mine Safety and Health Amendments Act, 1977
87. Black Lung Benefits Reform Act, 1977
88. Department of Energy Organization Act, 1977
89. Clean Water Act, 1977
90. Surface Mining Control and Reclamation Act, 1977
91. Fair Debt Collection Practices Act, 1977
92. Housing and Community Development Act, 1977
93. Community Reinvestment Act, 1977
94. Treasury Department Order No. 120-1, 1978
95. Neighborhood Self-Help Development Act, 1978
96. Liveable Cities Act, 1978
97. Customs Procedural Reform and Simplification Act, 1978
98. Trafficking in Contraband Cigarettes Act, 1978
99. Reorganization Plan No. 1, 1978
100. Pregnancy Discrimination Act, 1978
101. Civil Service Reform Act, 1978
102. Antarctic Conservation Act, 1978
103. Power Plant and Industrial Fuel Use Act, 1978
104. International Banking Act, 1978
105. Financial Institutions Regulatory and Interest Rate Control Act, 1978
106. National Credit Union Administration Central Liquidity Facility Act, 1978
107. Outer Continental Shelf Lands Act Amendments, 1978
108. Act of September 30, 1978
109. Airline Deregulation Act, 1978
110. Cargo Deregulation Act, 1978
111. Natural Gas Policy Act, 1978
112. Trade Agreements Act, 1979
113. Hazardous Liquid Pipeline Safety Act, 1979

114. Reorganization Plan No. 1, Executive Order No. 12142, 1979
115. Aviation Safety and Noise Abatement Act, 1979
116. International Air Transportation Act, 1979
117. Reorganization Plan No. 3, 1979
118. Federal Election Campaign Act Amendments, 1979
119. Export Administration Act, 1979
120. Crude Oil Windfall Profits Act, 1980
121. Comprehensive Environmental Response, Compensation and Liability Act, 1980
122. Depository Institutions Deregulation and Monetary Control Act, 1980
123. Motor Carrier Act, 1980
124. Staggers Rail Act, 1980
125. Federal Trade Commission Improvement Act, 1980*

* The above data have been grouped into decades to make them compatible with the decennial cycles of money growth and inflation examined in Chapters 3 and 4. Thus, each decade has eleven years, including the first and the last. This grouping procedure means that some regulatory acts appear twice in the data. Thus one can easily see how the following Table 3 is derived from Table 2.

APPENDIX

Table 3

Data Underlying Chart 6

Decades	No. of Regulatory Agencies per Decade	No. of Major Economic Laws per Decade
1760–1770		4
1770–1780		16
1780–1790		8
1790–1800		7
1800–1810		10
1810–1820		7
1820–1830		6
1830–1840	1	9
1840–1850	0	5
1850–1860	0	5
1860–1870	2	18
1870–1880	1	10
1880–1890	1	10
1890–1900	1	14
1900–1910	1	14
1910–1920	14	57
1920–1930	3	31
1930–1940	11	48
1940–1950	24	80
1950–1960	4	41
1960–1970	12	73
1970–1980	20	125

AUTHOR'S NOTE

THIS BOOK is a revised and updated edition of the one I wrote in 1984 under the same title, which was published by Venus Books, Dallas, Texas, in May 1985. My basic conclusions have not changed; they have, if anything, been reinforced by recent events. In the present edition, however, I have made an effort to clarify my argument and to present practical suggestions that we may follow, both as individuals and as a nation, to minimize the impact of the coming economic crisis.

The book, as with much of my recent work, is derived from the ideas of my mentor, P. R. Sarkar. I owe a great intellectual and inspirational debt to his prodigious work on economics and history, which lies at the heart of my investigation. I am also grateful to my friend and former student, Thor Thorgeirsson, for invaluable moral support and useful discussion on this subject. Many other students in my classes, notably Kathleen Adler, Jamal Abu Rashed, Asif Dowla, Matiur Rahman, and Nadeem Naqvi, deserve credit for the clarification of my ideas.

I have also benefited a great deal from discussions with my colleagues, Professors William Russell, Thomas Fomby, Phil Porter, Daniel Slottje, and Josef Hadar. Susan Meyn, who typed the manuscript, was invaluable to me. Thanks are also due to Ameri Trust Company for their permission to use their charts in Chapter 6.

I deeply appreciate the editorial assistance and wise counsel from Fred Hills, my editor at Simon and Schuster. He even collected some new data for me and helped me considerably in updating the previous edition of the book. Eileen Caughlin, my copy editor, did a superb job with the manuscript. I am also indebted to Jan Miller, my literary agent, who led me to Simon and Schuster.

Finally, there is my wife, Sunita, who had to draw the charts and diagrams and endure the drudgery of reading the manuscript again and again. For her understanding and fortitude, I am eternally grateful.

Ravi Batra

Dallas, Texas
November 1986

NOTES

1. See Bob Heeth, "Economics Expert Predicts Spread of War," *Nashville Banner,* Sept. 30, 1980; and "Professor Catches People's Attentions with Predictions," *The Tennessean,* Oct. 14, 1980.
2. Cf. Ravi Batra, *The Great Depression of 1990* (Dallas: Venus Books, 1985), pp. 143–144.
3. Ravi Batra, *Muslim Civilization and the Crisis in Iran* (Dallas: Venus Books, 1980).
4. P. R. Sarkar, *Human Society, Part 2* (Proutist Universal, 1354 Montague Street, N.W., Washington, D.C. 20011, 1967).
5. Ravi Batra, *Capitalism and Communism: A New Study of History* (London: Macmillan, 1978).
6. Sarkar, op. cit., p. 40.
7. See, for instance, Edward Burns and Phillip Ralph, *World Civilizations* (New York: W. W. Norton, 1974).
8. Paul Lacroix, *History of Prostitution* (New York: Covici Friede, 1931), pp. 6–7.
9. Batra, *Capitalism and Communism,* op. cit., chapter 5.
10. Charles A. and Mary R. Beard, *The Rise of American Civilization.* Vol. I (New York: Macmillan, 1925), pp. 109–110.

11. Gilbert Fite and Jim Reese, *An Economic History of the United States* (Boston: Houghton Mifflin, 1973), p. 355.
12. Milton Friedman and Anna Schwartz, *A Monetary History of the United States, 1867–1960* (Princeton, N.J.: Princeton University Press, 1963), p. 259.
13. John Gurley and Edward Shaw, "The Growth of Money and Debt in the United States," *Review of Economics and Statistics,* August 1957, p. 258.
14. This assumption is clearly unnecessary, but gives us an extra observation and helps with the visual appearance of the cycle developed in Chart 4. Such a procedure is not without precedent. Simon Kuznets often used it while converting his data into decade or five-year averages.
15. Credit for devising the indexes to quantify the degree of regulation, which is hard to measure, goes to Ronald Penoyer, who also provides much of the data presented in the appendix to Chapter 5.
16. Lindley Clark and Laurie McGinley, "Monetarists Succeed in Pushing Back Ideas But Not Their Policies," *Wall Street Journal,* Dec. 10, 1984.
17. Ralph Winter, "A Low Inflation Rate Can Be Painful," *Wall Street Journal,* Dec. 11, 1984.
18. John Kenneth Galbraith, *The Great Crash, 1929* (London: Hamish Hamilton, 1955), p. 156.
19. This table, minus the 1870, 1963, and 1983 figures, appears in Jonathan Turner and Charles Starnes, *Inequality: Privilege and Poverty in America* (Pacific Palisades, Calif.: Goodyear Publishing Company, 1976). The 1870 figure is obtained from Lee Soltow, *Men and Wealth in the United States, 1850–1870* (New Haven: Yale University Press, 1975). The 1963 and 1983 figures are obtained from the revised estimates provided by the Joint Economic Committee of Congress in 1986. These estimates are reported by Warren Brooks in *Insight,* Sept. 22, 1986, p. 49.
20. This is the celebrated Arrow-Pratt hypothesis of decreasing absolute risk aversion.
21. Charles Kindleberger, *Manias, Panics, and Crashes* (New York: Basic Books, 1978).
22. Jeffrey Williamson and Peter Lindert, *American Inequality: A Macroeconomic History* (New York: Academic Press, 1980), p. 46.
23. See, for instance, Christian Saint-Etienne, *The Great Depression, 1929–38: The Lesson for the 1980s* (Stanford, Calif.: Hoover Institution Press, 1984); Peter Temin, *Did Monetary Forces Cause the*

Great Depression? (New York: W. W. Norton, 1976); Karl Brunner, *The Great Depression Revisited* (New York: Martinus Nijhoff, 1981); Paul Volcker, *The Rediscovery of the Business Cycle* (New York: Free Press, 1978); and Charles Kindleberger, op. cit.

24. Rudiger Dornbusch and Stanley Fischer, *Macroeconomics,* 3rd ed. (New York: McGraw-Hill, 1983), p. 547.
25. Lindley Clark and Alfred Malabre, "Economists Don't See Threats to Economy Portending Depression," *Wall Street Journal,* Oct. 12, 1984.
26. See, for instance, Leonard Silk, "Need to Mesh World Policies," *New York Times,* July 16, 1986; Scott Burns, "Evaluating Depression Predictions," *Dallas Morning News,* Oct. 20, 1985; Barton Biggs, "Apocalypse Soon? The Great Depression of 1990," *Morgan Stanley Newsletter,* June 24, 1986; Marc Devries, "The Doomsday Scenario," *Town and Country,* October 1986; and John Kenneth Galbraith, "The 1929 Parallel," *Atlantic Monthly,* January 1987. Kenneth Boulding and Christian Saint-Etienne are other notable economists who believe that another depression can occur.
27. David Kotz, "How Many Billionaires Are Enough?" *New York Times,* Oct. 19, 1986.
28. Cf. David Shribman, "Economic Conditions in States Vary Dramatically As a Study Shows 31 Are Experiencing Recessions," *Wall Street Journal,* Aug. 26, 1986.
29. Irvine Sprague, *Bailout: An Insider's Account of Bank Failures and Rescues* (New York: Basic Books, 1986).
30. Peter Waldoman and William Celis III, "Severe Deflation Hits Commercial Properties in Many Areas of U.S.," *Wall Street Journal,* Sept. 4, 1986, p. 1.
31. Ravi Batra, *Prout: The Alternative to Capitalism and Marxism* (Proutist Universal, 1354 Montague Street, N.W., Washington, D.C. 20011, 1980).
32. The breakup of American Telephone and Telegraph in 1985 is a prime example of dividing monopolies into smaller competing units. As a result, long-distance phone rates have come down sharply.

INDEX

Index

ABOUT THE AUTHOR

ONE OF the top trade theorists in the world, Dr. Ravi Batra is Professor of Economics at Southern Methodist University, where he received his appointment at age 30 to a full professorship and served as Chairman of the Economics Department from 1977 to 1980. He was ranked third in a group of 46 "superstars" selected from all the economists at American and Canadian universities by the learned journal *Economic Inquiry* (October 1978). Dr. Batra is the author of numerous articles on international economic problems and seven books, including *Studies in the Pure Theory of International Trade* and *Theory of International Trade Under Uncertainty.*